"A wonderfully written account of a family's fencing legacy written by a son paying tribute to his dad. *Closing the Distance* is a heartfelt journey that shouldn't be missed."

—Robert Spivak
Chairman, Maccabi USA/Sports for Israel

"This father son journey engages readers in a rich landscape of touching stories that moves from trials, tribulations, and tears to triumphs. Jeff entertains us with brutally honest humor and tons of heart. Every page will bring you closer to finding the energy to chase and fulfill your own dreams."

—Terrence L. Gargiulo
President of MAKINGSTORIES.net,
author of On Cloud Nine, Stories at Work,
and the Strategic Use of Stories

"Jeff's fascinating story is a journey of personal discovery gilded in the unique mystique of the fencing world."

—Eric Rosenberg
past President, New York Fencers Club

"Jeff Bukantz's autobiography has a personal interest to me, since his father and I were close friends and roommates on many of the international events and at least two Olympic Games, where we refereed together. I followed Jeff's carreer as a fencer and referee and was very pleased to see his progress in both, achieving national and international fame. This of course is stepping in his father's shoes, except for the one step he outpaced him by becoming Captain of the National and Olympic Team. I congratulate Jeff on his book, reading it with great pleasure, bringing many great and pleasant memories back to me as well."

—Chaba M. Pallaghy
past Vice-President of the International Fencing Federation
and Chair of the FIE Arbitrage Commission

CLOSING THE DISTANCE

Chasing a Father's
Olympic Fencing Legacy

Jeff Bukantz

"I love the personal stories behind the stats and headlines. Jeff Bukantz has seen it all as the son of an international fencing icon, as a national champion himself, and as captain of the US Olympic Team. His memoir is not only important reading, it's fascinating."

–Joe Siegman
author, Jewish Sports Legends

"The Bukantz father and son are a fencing phenomenon. Now son (Jeff) has written a memoir that is a touching tribute to his father (Dan) as well as a highly readable account of one fencer's education both on the strip and far beyond. However, those who like their reading to be decorous and free from controversy are advised to stay away from this book."

–Richard Cohen
author, By The Sword

"A compelling and heartfelt journey through the Bukantz family fencing legacy."

–Doug Herzog
President, Spike TV and Comedy Central

"Jeff Bukantz has written an emotional and fascinating tribute, both to family love and unity and to the work ethic that goes into becoming a world-class competitor. *Closing the Distance* is wonderful reading for anyone whether or not they are interested in sports."

–Ron Carner
Vice-President, Maccabi USA/Sports for Israel
18th Maccabiah General Chairman

"Jeff's candid portrayal of his against-all-odds journey is the ultimate inspiration for anyone who has dared to dream."

–Carl Borack
Olympian and four-time Olympic Fencing Captain

"I think that this is a wonderfully written book about a boy's love and admiration for his father. It has a wonderful flow; it captures your interest as soon as you pick up the book. I loved it."

—Peter Westbrook
six-time US Olympian, Olympic Bronze Medalist in Fencing,
author, Harnessing Anger

"I enjoyed covering Jeff at the Athens Olympics in 2004. Until now, I didn't realize what it really meant to him to be there – namely, the culmination of a journey – the realization of a dream. This book serves as a poignant reminder of what perseverance is all about. *Closing the Distance* is both inspirational and emotional. It is a brilliantly woven story of the relationship between father and son, and how pressure and expectations can be handled with class. Jeff Bukantz has long proven to be both a 'giant' and a 'gem' in the sports industry and this book is a winner."

—Bruce Beck
WNBC-TV Sports Anchor/Reporter

"I was surprised at how much Jeff was in touch with his father. Jeff is a very talented man, and he was proud of his father without ever showing any sort of inferiority complex."

—Semyon (Simon) Pinkhasov
Fencing coach

"Anyone who has had a close and rewarding relationship with his father, as I had, will thrill with understanding as he reads Jeff's splendid story."

—Sid Dorfman
Hall of Fame Sportswriter

"Charming, insightful, and fabulously interesting."
—Alan Sherman
Chairman, International Jewish Sports Hall of Fame

"When I became the first American to military press five hundred-pounds, it was just me versus the weight. That weight was nothing compared to the burden Jeff carried on his shoulders, where it was Jeff versus his father's legacy. What an uplifting story!"
—Ken Patera
Olympian and former "World's Strongest Man"

"As both of my parents are Olympians, I know the pressure Jeff faced. His emotional journey, described with his usual candor, offers a heartwarming and humorous look at the struggle to make your own mark on the world."
—Mariel Zagunis
member of the 2004 US Olympic Fencing Team,
and the first US Olympic Gold Medalist in Fencing since 1904

CLOSING THE DISTANCE

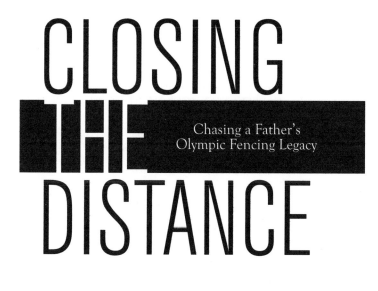

Chasing a Father's
Olympic Fencing Legacy

Jeff Bukantz

ACANTHUS
PUBLISHING

Boston, Massachusetts
www.AcanthusPublishing.com

Published by Acanthus Publishing,
a division of The Ictus Group, LLC
343 Commercial Street
Unit 214, Union Wharf
Boston, MA 02109

Grateful acknowledgement is made for permission to reprint portions of the following
copyrighted materials: "During one foil at the national championships, Jeffrey Bukantz
of New York..." by John Dart, *Los Angeles Times*, June 27, 1984; *By the Sword* by
Richard Cohen (Random House, 2002); MaccabiUSA.com.

We also acknowledge permission to reproduce the following copyrighted images:
American Fencing magazine, June 1958 & 1991 covers; photograph of 2004 Olympic
opening ceremonies provided by Getty Images; photographs provided by Robert
Largman, Michael Spivak of MaccabiUSA/Sports for Israel, Serge Timacheff of
fencingphotos.com, and Alice Bukantz.

Publisher's Cataloging-in-Publication Data
(Prepared by The Donohue Group, Inc.)

Bukantz, Jeff.
    Closing the distance: chasing a father's Olympic fencing legacy /
    Jeff Bukantz. -- 1st ed.

    p. : ill ; cm.

    ISBN-13: 978-1-933631-30-1
    ISBN-10: 1-933631-30-9

    1. Bukantz, Jeff. 2. Bukantz, Daniel.
    3. Fencers--United States--Biography.
    I. Title.

GV1144.2.B85 B85 2006
796.8/6/092

ISBN-10: 1-933631-30-9
ISBN-13: 978-1-933631-30-1

Cover Design: Anthony Manes
Cover Photo: Jeff (on the right) scoring against 8-time US National Champion Mike
            Marx with "The Blaster" to the flank at the 1981 Nationals held in Fort
            Worth, Texas at Texas Christian University's Daniel-Meyer Coliseum.
Interior Layout: Julie Reilly

DEDICATION

*To Dad, who gently nudged me into
the sport we both love so dearly.*

*To Mom, who gave me the drive to
succeed no matter what the obstacles.*

*To my wife Carol, who supported my quest
despite the family hardships it caused.*

*To my children, Stephanie and Michael,
who saved our relationships by not becoming
third-generation fencing Bukantzes.*

Table of Contents

1

Danny Bukantz's Son

Just a few months before I was born, Danny Bukantz won his fourth United States National Foil Championship in Milwaukee. And before that, he represented his country in the 1948, 1952, and 1956 Olympic Games.

The die had been cast. Whether or not I was to follow in his footsteps, I would forever be known in the fencing community as Danny Bukantz's son.

And you know what? I always thought that was pretty cool.

At a young age I met many important fencers who were friends of my parents. From time to time, Dad would bring me to major fencing competitions. These occasions were different sorts of double-edged swords; while he was proud to show me off to his world, I was always just as proud to have a dad who was so well known, respected, and loved in the fencing community.

One of my earliest memories from that time goes back to the 1964 US Nationals held at Atlantic City's Convention Center located right on the boardwalk. During a break from the competition, I was walking on the famed wooden walkway with Dad and his buddy, Ed Richards. Ed had come into the tournament as the defending National Champion, but had just been dethroned.

So it was a very sad stroll on the New Jersey promenade that day. I remember Ed looking so down in the dumps; as a seven-year-old, all I could think to console him with was, "Hey, Ed, you can't win 'em all."

I've heard this story a hundred times – Ed still relates it to me when we see each other. He and Dad both say it broke the tension and temporarily pulled Ed out of his doldrums. I guess sometimes the truth, especially when delivered by a youngster who doesn't know any better, is the best medicine.

Ed Richards is just one of the many colorful characters I've learned to love as the years have gone by. No matter where I'd go, people in the fencing community would always say such incredible things about my dad.

"Oh, you should have seen it when your dad beat Jean-Claude Magnan at the Martini and Rossi event at the New York Athletic Club!," one of his many fencing friends once told me. As it turned out, in 1961, when Dad was already an old-timer at the age of 44, he drew the 22-year-old fencing star in the quarterfinal round of eight. (Magnan went on to win the 1963 and 1965 World Championships. He won the silver medal at the 1964 Olympics.)

As Dad tells his side of the story, "I didn't expect to have a chance, so before the match I went up to the dining room, had a big steak and a bottle of wine."

Danny Bukantz was a cerebral fencer who's been known to rely on a bear-trap defense, and for the match-up against Magnan he knew his only game plan would be to stay within his strength. As I've been told by many who witnessed the bout, Dad "stuck out his ample belly, almost as a lure, drew Magnan in to attack, and at the last minute parried his thrust and hit him with a perfect riposte."

Dad always adds, "I let him chase me – until I caught him!"

Though I wasn't at the famous match, I can clearly envision the great moment. Mostly because there are still those – more than four decades later – who were there and love to relate the story to me.

As the years went by, Dad retired from competition and devoted his time to refereeing. He wasn't just any old referee – he became known as the best in the country as well as one of the best in the world. He refereed at a record five Olympics.

I was the son of a full-fledged American legend in the sport of fencing. While I loved every moment of adulation Dad received, early on I didn't have the drive to follow in his sizable footsteps. I'm not sure why. Maybe I was unmotivated or thought the drive would come whenever I felt I was ready. Maybe I felt my pedigree would guarantee greatness.

Maybe I was afraid. (Why would I have been? Well, try to imagine you are Michael Jordan's son. Wayne Gretzky's... Jack Nicklaus's...)

Whatever the case, I never developed the urge to jump into fencing when I was younger. Sure, Dad would take me down to the New York Fencers Club, a place as iconic as he was. The NYFC, established in 1883, is the oldest and largest fencing club in the western hemisphere. At that time, there were two other prominent and highly successful clubs in New York City, Salle Santelli and the New York Athletic Club.

There was a huge intra-city rivalry among the three clubs, and each would angle to get the best young fencers in the city to join them. When Dad was the hottest foil fencer in the country, he was invited by the bigwigs of the NYAC to join their prestigious club. He arrived at the interview with an open mind about joining, only to be told – in no uncertain terms – to put down on his application form that he was *not* Jewish.

He was, naturally, aghast. Despite what members of the NYAC would later claim, this was the normal operating procedure at the notoriously anti-Semitic club. Although the times have changed at this once anti-everything-not-WASP institution, Dad's terrible experience would forever make my skin crawl when I walked into that building, and would come to play a role in a major decision I would have to make later in my life.

Ironically, Dad got his revenge against the NYAC. He was running the Metropolitan Championships at the NYAC in 1949, but there was a problem: the NYAC didn't want to allow a black fencer to compete. Dad refused to hold the competition until this decision was revoked. The Metropolitan Section board held a meeting, and after all sorts of pressure the NYAC was forced to back down.

It was the epitome of poetic justice. Dad's steadfast resolve forced the club that had insisted he deny his Judaism to allow all black fencers to compete at their facility.

Back to the original point. Dad would drag me to his all-inclusive club – the NYFC – to fence. While he was careful not to push me onto the strip – as he assumed (correctly) I'd resent it – he still wanted me to get a taste of the sport. He had picked up his first foil when he was 15; I was roughly the same age, but, as you'll come to see, we experienced very different results.

Both of us are lefties, so I was able to use his foils. After showing me the en garde position and some basic foot and handwork, he'd give me a short lesson. These were the mirror image of the lessons given to him and every other fencer by his coaches and involved repetitive drilling of simple technical moves over some twenty minutes.

The *en garde* position is the basic stance in fencing. You start by putting your heels together at a perpendicular "L" shape and then you move your feet about a shoulder's width apart; the toe of your lead foot (which corresponds with your fencing hand) points at your opponent. Then you squat down about halfway – your knees should be bent at an angle greater than forty-five but less than ninety degrees. The objective of the en garde position is to keep your balance centered so you can move forward (*advance*) and backward (*retreat*) with equal ease. Think of an infielder on the baseball diamond centering his stance to move either left or right to grab a ground ball.

Dad, thankfully, wasn't too big a nitpicker when he began showing me the ropes. If he had been, I would have likely been turned off from fencing forever. He worked with me on simple moves and gave me plenty of positive reinforcement.

In fencing there are offensive moves and defensive moves. I learned the defensive ones first, *parries*. A parry blocks your opponent's attack. The *four parry* protects your inside target, which is basically most of your torso. The *six parry* protects your outside target, which is mostly your flank. There are plenty more where that came from, but for a beginning fencer that's probably enough.

The sport of fencing is often likened to physical chess. Your opponent will try to avoid your parry with a move called a *disengage*, which is when the point (the tip) of the sword is dropped under the parry. The bout continues until one of the fencers scores a *touch* (or point).

Now, while Dad is a living, breathing encyclopedia of fencing knowledge, terminology, and technique, he always kept his lessons with me simple. Instead of laying tons of minutiae on me, he focused on an aspect of fencing that he felt was *the* single most important one, the one that ultimately separates the also-rans from the champions – "**keeping your distance.**"

No matter how fast a fencer is, how good his or her technique, or how experienced – it would all be for naught without the ability to keep the distance, which means the space between you and your opponent during the bout. As you advance and retreat, your objective is to create a situation where you put yourself inside your opponent's distance. This technique will enable you to score a touch. Of course, it's equally important to prevent your opponent from getting into your distance. It's tricky; the best fencers seem to have a sixth sense about the right distance to keep.

When my dad beat Magnan – a guy half his age – it was all about his uncanny ability to irritate the world champion by keeping a perfect distance and finally frustrating him into making mistakes.

Recently I traveled to Leipzig, Germany where I was Team Captain for the United States Fencing Team at the World Championships. The women's foil champion, Italy's Valentina Vezzali, also won the Olympic gold in Athens in 2004. She has won more World Cup competitions in the last ten years than any fencer in any weapon. Simply put: She is unbeatable. But Vezzali is, without a doubt, the most boring fencer I've ever watched. She isn't flashy; she doesn't attack often – she is simply difficult to hit. And there's one reason for her dominance: *distance*. Vezzali has the innate ability to keep perfect distance from her opponents.

So, the greatest women's foil fencer in history credits "keeping the distance" as her #1 weapon of choice. I guess Dad was onto something when he constantly harped on me about keeping the distance.

Whenever I see parents and coaches on the sidelines barking all sorts of specific advice to their fencers, I think back to when I was beginning. Dad would sit at the end of the strip (where all the action happens, about fourteen meters long and two meters wide), usually smoking a cigarette, and watch my bouts. I can only imagine what he was going through, hoping his only son would win, but at the same time becoming ultra-frustrated because I couldn't fence as well or as naturally as he did.

But no matter how things were progressing on the strip, no matter how badly I wanted some coaching gem to help me out, Dad would always reassure me by saying, "Keep your distance," or "Keep the legs moving."

It may have seemed like generic advice, but it really was

profound. Without adhering to his mantras, I was a dead duck. When I kept my distance and my legs moving, I always had a chance to score a touch.

As the teaching process progressed, Dad imparted some specific tactical and technical moves. One of these eventually became my specialty, what I was known for as I entered the competitive scene.

Dad taught me a different parry called *counter four* or *circle four*. When an opponent tries to disengage from your original four parry, you make a circle in the clockwise direction (if you're a lefty like me – you righties would circle counterclockwise) and return your blade to where it was after your initial four parry. Basically, this move has the effect of catching your opponent's blade if she or he tries to avoid the four parry with a disengage.

Of course, your opponent might avoid your counter four with another disengage – that's just how the sport works. However, if done correctly – and from the proper distance – the counter four parry is deadly. And, as Dad worked on this critical move with me, it became my bread and butter.

After a successful counter four parry, I would make my own offensive action – known as a *riposte*. The whole purpose of these moves linked together was to utilize a bear-trap defense as a means of turning a defensive action into an offensive one.

I'll never forget the time I faced a fencer from New Jersey who was coached by John Geraci. Geraci, a friend of Dad's (who wasn't?), had scouted my earlier bouts that day and proclaimed that his fencer would easily circumvent my signature counter four parry. I remember that Dad, always a modest man who never talked trash or bragged, responded brashly to Geraci, "Let him try." After Geraci walked away, Dad turned to me and said, "If you keep your distance, he won't have a chance." I did… And he didn't.

Again, keeping the distance was Dad's primary and practical tactic. It was reassuring, though, to have Dad instill in me that what had become the bread and butter of my game would succeed as long as I kept that damn distance.

When looking back on our father-son relationship as coach and protégé, I realize how incredibly important the distance mantra was to my success. While most parents and coaches were forever searching for the magic elixir – the special move that would bring fencing success – the one who knew all the tricks instinctively knew that "keeping the distance" was the most important.

You might not be surprised to hear that Dad and I quickly learned how difficult it is for a parent and a child to work together in these types of situations. Later in life, when my son Michael acted up while I tried to teach him baseball or tennis, I harkened back to the days when I was the same stubborn offspring, and I backed off. I learned to do that from Dad, who realized that the father-son relationship, no matter how close, just wasn't the ideal teaching scenario. So he pushed me onto two of his friends, Nat Lubell and Frank Bavuso. Uncle Nat, as I called him, worked with me whenever I came down to the club. He was a patient coach and an Olympian, and he had grown up on the same block in the Bronx as Dad. We hit it off right away. Frank, although not an Olympian, was a genteel coach to whom I also related.

Every now and then, Dad would still give me a workout. Inevitably, the teenager in me would insist I knew better than him and start acting up. Dad, an uncharacteristically patient man, was probably frustrated as hell. There he was, the great fencer, simply trying to pass along some of his wealth of experience and breadth of knowledge to his pride and joy. The only problem was that little Jeffrey was no joy to work with.

While Dad emphasized keeping the distance and usually schooled me on the basics of fencing, he would occasionally try to show me some of his special moves. Like the time he tried to teach me the action called *absence of blade*. This move involves pressing your blade against your opponent's, who should instinctively react by pushing back. At that moment, you pull your blade toward your body, basically disengaging yourself from your opponent's blade. As that happens, your opponent's momentum from pushing back on your blade (which is no longer there) causes his or her blade to be in a temporarily defenseless position, and that presents a split second for you to hit an open target.

In order to accomplish this tactic, you and your opponent would have to be fencing at a close distance. Here, blade work is constant, which is why this is the only way the move can work. But there was a problem, at least as I saw it. After all, I was a teenager, and teenagers always know more than their parents. Even in this case!

The problem was that the current style of fencing was done at a longer distance. In Dad's era the fencers faced off closer to one another. That era was known for its "conversation of the blades," as fencers constantly engaged one another's blade.

So I told him matter-of-factly while we worked on the move, "Dad, this will never work." I know he was frustrated because he knew better. But he persisted and we continued to practice the (in my mind) totally outdated action. And every time we did, like a petulant child I would always say in my most condescending tone, "Dad, this will never work."

I never once intentionally tried that move in a bout. After all, it'd never work in the modern era of fencing. However, as my career evolved, I realized that absence of blade would become one of the most important moves in my repertoire.

And how did that happen? As it turns out, I just started doing a version of the action without thinking. Even in the longer-distanced modern fencing, there were plenty of times when the fencers would be at a close distance and their blades engaged. Instinctively, I would do the absence of blade move, and I usually scored a touch.

The tactic I had believed would never work was actually the magical tactic that scored a lot of touches. Dad was right.

And, because he was always persistent enough to keep teaching his wiseass son, the move became one that I would do without thinking. I have to admit that I was shocked when I realized the move's effectiveness. I couldn't wait to get home from the competition where this epiphany occurred and tell Dad that he was right after all. I revered him and had no problem admitting I was wrong. (Well, this one time anyway…) I was just so happy for him. After the way I argued with him every time he worked on the absence of blade action, he deserved an unconditional "You were right, Dad!"

It was probably during this time that I felt the combination of my bloodline and early foray into the sport would automatically lead me to enormous second-generation success. I worked out every once in a while and just assumed that I was on the fast track to greatness.

When I started Forest Hills High School as a sophomore in 1971, I never thought of going out for the fencing team. I wasn't even sure that I wanted to go into competitive fencing at that point. It was like I was reluctant to get a start in the sport: I was scared to death of trying to follow in Danny Bukantz's giant footsteps.

What I do know is that despite practicing at the best fencing club in New York City, getting lessons from Dad and his superstar friends, and trying to be the world's biggest jock, I didn't once consider joining the high school team.

Well, my junior year all that changed. I was daydreaming during gym class as the teacher, Lenny Messitte, took attendance. Out of nowhere, he started asking for recruits to the fencing team. I didn't consider it for a second. Then he looked at me and blurted out, "Hey, Bukantz! I hear you fence. You better get your fat ass to the tryouts."

That, ladies and gentlemen, was the first defining moment of my fencing career. It wasn't my choice, it wasn't glamorous, but rather public peer pressure from the high school's fencing coach. It wasn't that I was the great offspring of the legendary

Danny Bukantz, but rather a "fat ass."

It was the beginning of what would be a humbling experience.

Although I immediately thought I was the greatest thing to happen to fencing since it'd been electrified, I learned in rapid fashion that I was anything but. In fact, I was only the fourth best out of the six-man team that first year. And worse, I was so fat that I could barely fit into my fencing jacket.

And while it was cool to be accepted so easily into the fencing family at such a young age, that acceptance meant nothing once I started competing. Not only would my name *not* instill fear into my opponents, in some cases, it would give them more incentive to stick me senseless.

I had a bull's-eye on my back and a chip on my shoulder.

In fact, this is exactly what happened during a high school match in 1972. I may have been the kin of a fencing legend, but I was also a neophyte, not very good, and more than a little pudgy. As soon as the fencers from Cardozo High School caught wind of my last name and its connection to Olympic greatness, they set out to destroy me. Which they did. I lost both of my bouts badly that day. And – to boot – it was the first time Dad ever watched me fence competitively.

It was a Friday afternoon at Benjamin Cardozo High School in Queens. For Dad, Friday was always golf day, a deserved break from his midtown Manhattan dental practice, but he made it to the auditorium just in time for my first bout against Mitch Dorfman, a guy half my size, three times as fast, and, quite frankly, ten times better. As Dad watched from the stands, Dorfman destroyed me, 5-1. As you can imagine, I felt as low as humanly possible. To make matters worse, the bout's referee, Olympian Marty Lang, made his way over to my end of the strip and said, in clear earshot of Dad, "Bukantz, you couldn't hit the side of a barn!"

How ironic that the meet would be held on the raised stage of the Cardozo auditorium. I was knocked right off the pedestal I had envisioned myself on; the fall was that much farther.

My second bout and second loss was against Eric Rosenberg, who actually became one of my best friends later in life. He was the one who eventually told me about the Cardozo fencers and their desire to show up the fat son of Danny Bukantz in his first competitive outing.

Over the next fifteen years, Rosenberg and I traveled around the country and the world competing in tournaments. Between practice and competition, we've probably fenced each other hundreds of times. And – to put it nicely – I avenged this loss in some of the most important bouts of my career.

These early high school competitions were definitely reality checks. True to form, Dad never piled on the pressure. Instead, he advised me in the areas I had to work on and promised to help me improve whenever I wanted. His was a loving style that I now employ with my own son, though I tend to be somewhat critical. Dad was never, *ever*, critical of me.

Sometime during that first competitive season, I fenced in an historic bout.

I was trailing my opponent, 0-4. Quite frankly, I didn't think I could ever come back from such a deficit. I'd never done it and it seemed like an impossible task. If this guy was good enough to hit me four times in a row, how on God's Green Earth could I come back to win?

I evaluated my technique and realized I wasn't keeping my distance. I was too close. I was letting this guy get the better of me. So, going back to the never-fail mantra of Danny Bukantz, I decided to start keeping the distance. I also stayed within my defensive game and scored on five straight ripostes.

I did the seemingly impossible! I came back to win the match 5-4. I was so proud; I couldn't wait to tell Dad when he arrived home from work. He finally walked through the door with his fedora atop his head and *The New York Post* folded under his arm.

"Hey, Dad, listen to this!" I said, swelled with pride. "I was down 0-4 in this bout today, but came back and beat the guy!"

Without missing a beat, he made his own winning riposte: "Schmuck! How did you let the guy get a 4-0 lead in the first place?!"

I had my work cut out for me. Dad was a living legend, a lovable guy, a four-time Olympian, a four-time individual National Champion, a nine-time team National Champion, the highest rated international referee, and World Maccabiah Champion in 1950.

I could barely win a high school bout.

Going into it, though, I knew that it would be nearly impossible to duplicate his career, let alone any of his competitive or refereeing accomplishments. But I set my bar high. Every fencer dreams of winning a national championship and competing in the Olympics. But I also dreamed of following in my father's footsteps. Both dreams went hand in hand; I was taking on a monumental task. I knew that, too.

But, while I did so willingly – and while Dad never pushed me (well, maybe a few "nudges") – I was getting myself into a no-win scenario. Anything less than a national championship or a spot on an Olympic Team would render me a failure of sorts. At least that's how I looked at it. It was a daunting and scary hill to climb.

Dad spent his time reassuring me that whatever I accomplished in the fencing world would be great, and that he was just so proud of me for even trying my hand at the sport. I listened, I believed him, and his words took some edge off my worries about following in his footsteps.

But let's be honest: I spent the next thirty-five years trying.

2

Danny Bukantz

Daniel Bukantz was born on December 4, 1917. He was the youngest of three siblings; his big brother Samuel was born in 1911 and middle sister Dorothy was born in 1913. The three were the children of Bertha and Barnett, who originally came to America from Lithuania. Barnett, in fact, left Lithuania in 1903 about two weeks before the Czar came through his small town.

The Bukantz family lived in an apartment at 1955 Grand Concourse and 178th Street, about a mile from Yankee Stadium. As a youngster, Danny was an all-around athlete. He played all the usual city sports like handball, stickball, baseball, and basketball. Two of his friends, however, were doing something that was fairly foreign to most city kids; they were fencing. Harold Newton, who lived in the same apartment building as Danny, was the first one to try the sport. Nathaniel Lubell, who lived a block over at 179th off the concourse, was next.

Danny, fifteen at the time, ridiculed his friends and

claimed they were involved in a "sissy sport." So they challenged him to a duel – his first duel – but it was more like talking him into trying out the "sissy sport" just once. As he recounted to me, "I'll never forget the first time I fenced with Harold and Nat... I couldn't walk for a week!"

Once he could walk again, Danny decided to go back and give fencing another try, as he knew then that it was anything but a "sissy sport." He took to it like Senator Chuck Schumer takes to a television camera. He was hooked.

Danny graduated from DeWitt Clinton High School in the Bronx before he turned sixteen because he was bright enough to have skipped two whole grades. He attended the City College of New York (CCNY) and joined the fencing team.

CCNY used to have one of the best fencing teams in the country and produced a disproportionate amount of Olympic fencers over the years. Cornel Wilde actually fenced at CCNY a couple years ahead of Danny. Among his coaches at CCNY were Joe Montague, Joe Vince, and world-famous Olympic medalist Aldo Nadi.

Aldo Nadi was considered by fencing experts to be the greatest swordsman of all time. In addition to winning three Olympic gold medals, Nadi was well known for partaking in actual duels with rapiers, the precursor to the modern-day epee. He was a perfectionist and a disciplinarian, two traits that no doubt helped him become the undefeated European champion for twelve consecutive years.

Nadi also became a world-renowned fencing master, which is a fancy term for highly trained professional coach. His credentials as a competitor, duelist, and master were only surpassed by his gargantuan ego. His most famous quote: "I am the greatest fencer to ever live."

While Nadi earned legendary status in his native Italy, he decided to come to the United States in 1935 to make a living teaching fencing. He opened his own school in New York

City. In 1938, the coach of the CCNY fencing team, Joseph Vince, took ill. He asked Nadi to fill in for him at the college. Amazingly, Aldo Nadi, the self-proclaimed "greatest fencer in history," became the part-time coach for the City College of New York fencing team.

When Nadi met the team at practice, he wanted to put on an exhibition. Now, let me emphasize the word *he*. *He* wanted to show these collegiate fencers just why he called himself "the greatest fencer to ever live."

Danny, who had been fencing for about six years at this point, was a senior and captain of the fencing team. Naturally, Nadi chose him to be the guinea pig.

Well, Danny was the greatest *Bukantz fencer* to ever live.

They saluted, put on their masks, and began the ten-touch bout. Nadi went all out to establish who was the boss and hit Danny on the first touch. Then, in a patronizing show of sportsmanship, he "allowed" Danny to score the next touch. It was obvious to everyone watching that Nadi gave Danny the freebie as a show of good faith.

But that was the end of the niceties.

On the very next action, Nadi tried to steamroll Dad with the same explosive attack that scored the first touch. Only Danny retreated an extra bit of distance, parried, and riposted right to the middle of Nadi's chest.

The "greatest fencer to ever live" was shocked. He took off his mask and announced, "I am hit. You have hit the master."

As Dad related the story to me, "He probably scored the next nine touches, but I can tell you one thing: it was the greatest touch I ever scored."

Danny was also coached by Giorgio Santelli and Rene Pinchart. Danny credits Pinchart as being the best coach of the group and the one who made the greatest impact on his fencing technique and style.

After CCNY, Danny entered the New York University Dental School, which almost didn't happen. The Rabbi from Danny's temple felt very strongly that Danny had the aptitude to become a Rabbi. He put the pressure on Danny (a.k.a. Jewish guilt), but fortunately Barnett intervened and recommended a dental career.

Dad told me once, "If my father hadn't gotten involved, I probably would have become a Rabbi."

Oh, by the way, while at NYU Dental, Danny set the record for the most points in a basketball game. He was always a stellar athlete.

Before graduating in 1944, Danny had already been assigned to the 87th Infantry. Immediately after graduation, he was off to become a part of General Patton's 3rd Army. Danny and 18,000 others crammed into cabins for the journey on the Queen Elizabeth to England. As part of the right flank, Dad's brigade was eventually knee-deep in one of the worst (in terms of casualties) battles of World War II: the Battle of the Bulge.

On the day my mom was liberated from the concentration camp, Dad's unit was stationed nearby. To this day, Mom swears that she saw this handsome American soldier who she thinks was Dad.

When he returned home from war, Danny was among the honored servicemen and women who marched down Manhattan's Canyon of Heroes for a ticker-tape parade. The next time he would take that storied route was as a member of the United States Olympic Team.

After falling back into his normal life, Danny opened his dental practice and resumed his fencing training in the evenings. He was a member of the Saltus Club and Salle Montague for a while, but Danny eventually landed at the New York Fencers Club in 1948, a club that produced more Olympians than any other American fencing club.

As a dentist, Danny was cut from a different mold. He was primarily concerned with his patients, not his bank account. He treated many people who didn't have the means to pay for even the smallest treatment. Mom used to yell at him to charge more than he was charging, even to the full-paying patients. Sound corny? Maybe, but true nevertheless.

While Danny had patients in the chair – and at his mercy – he had a virtual encyclopedia of jokes he would tell. Most people fear going to the dentist; Danny's patients actually looked forward to their visits.

I know I enjoyed going to see him. Then again, I'd feel no pain while flying under the laughing gas (nitrous oxide).

As for fencing, Danny got back to his pre-war level and made the 1948 Olympic Team destined for London. He made his second voyage to England across the Atlantic on the Queen Elizabeth, a considerably more pleasant journey for Danny and his other teammates who had fought overseas.

But as Dad tells the tale, "I had better accommodations on the ship on the way to the War. For the Olympics, I roomed with Nat Lubell and Gus Prokop. They put us in the back of the boat, on the bottom deck, right above the screws. Those damn things made a terrible noise all the time. Those four or five days were boring, but at least I won a good amount of money playing poker with the guys."

Thanks to Danny's outstanding 15-1 record (doubly outstanding considering that Olympic Team captain Warren Dow told Nat Lubell that there wouldn't be a place for Danny on the team), the Men's 1948 Olympic Fencing Team finished fourth, just missing a medal.

Danny won his first US National Foil Championship in 1949.

In 1950, Danny was part of the US team that departed for Israel and the 3rd World Maccabiah Games. Thankfully, this trip was aboard a Trans World Airlines plane and not the Queen Elizabeth. The 1950 Maccabiah Games were an important event, as they were the first Jewish Games since the State of Israel was born and the first since they were halted in

1938 due to the Holocaust.

While Danny won the gold medal in the foil competition (defeating future World Champion Allan Jay along the way), he considered it far more meaningful, as a Jew, to have shown his solidarity by participating in Israel at the time.

*   *   *

In 1950 Dad became King of the Jews, but he would soon be chosen to compete against the best in the world.

In 1951, Jehan Buhan of France, gold medalist in foil at the 1948 Olympics, came to the United States to compete in the Martini & Rossi competition. While he was in NYC, a special exhibition was arranged before a black-tie only crowd at the Fencers Club. As the American champ and top dog at the club, Danny was Buhan's obvious opponent. As Dad told me, "Buhan and I went toe to toe, and neither one of us outscored the other. He beat me in London in 1948, but I felt pretty comfortable against him."

In 1956, a similar black-tie exhibition was arranged at the Fencers Club between Frenchman Christian D'Oriola, who won the Olympic gold medal in 1952 and 1956, and Dad. In Dad's opinion, "There was only one fencer in the world I didn't feel I could beat, at least consistently. That was D'Oriola." When I asked if it was a styles clash, Dad said, "No, it wasn't that. It was simply that he was, in my opinion, heads and tails above everyone else. He was just a great, great fencer.

"As for the exhibition," Dad continued, "we gave the audience a great show. We went back and forth and scored a similar amount of touches. However, I do believe that D'Oriola was fully capable of outscoring me if he really wanted to."

(The closest I came to being in Dad's shoes was in 1987 at the World Championships in Lausanne, when I fenced 1980 Olympic Silver medalist Pascal Jolyot, also from France. Thanks to the pre-match advice of Eric Rosenberg, I beat Jolyot 5-0 and knocked him out of the competition.)

In 1952 Danny won his second US National Foil Championship and was eager for another shot at the Olympics. Tragically, his sister Dorothy contracted an illness and passed away prior to the Games. In February 2006, I asked him how the sudden death of his older sister had weighed on him.

"Jeff," he answered, "I've never said this to anyone until now. I was in the best physical shape of my career and I honestly felt that I had a chance to win a medal. There is no question my performance was hampered by the mental anguish I had endured during my sister's illness. I had to be strong for her, for me, and also for my parents."

Though he didn't win an Olympic medal, in 1953 Danny successfully defended the title of US Champion, his third championship in five years. As he related this streak to me, "It was really four titles in those five years. At the 1951 Nationals in Detroit, I lost to Silvio Giolito 4-5 and took second in the competition. But I really hit him on the deciding touch, although I didn't get the call. A few years ago, after kidding Giolito about this, he finally said, 'Okay, Danny, you really won.'"

In 1956 Danny earned a spot on his third consecutive US Olympic Team. And again his outstanding record helped propel the team to another fourth-place result, just missing that elusive Olympic medal for the second time.

In 1957 Danny won his fourth US National Foil Championship in Milwaukee and eagerly awaited my birth in mid-October. In what must have been the most heart-wrenching period of his life, his father Barnett passed away suddenly just two weeks before I was born prematurely on September 17th.

Upon seeing little Jeffrey, Nat Lubell, one of Danny's oldest friends, remarked that I looked like a "Chinaman." My mother wouldn't speak to him for over a year. Well, as a jaundiced preemie, I can say that I did look like a scrawny chicken. Mom still shows me the picture of baby Jeff in a large pot taking a bath. Hmm... Maybe that's why I always refused to eat her pot roast.

In 1958 Danny represented the United States at the World Championships, which were held that year in Philadelphia. It was there that he accomplished a rare feat that is still talked about by the old-timers.

The Soviet Union boasted a line-up of Victor Zhdanovich, Yury Sisikin, Mark Midler, and German Sveshnikov. In the round of eight of the team match – the quarterfinals – Danny defeated all four Russians. The US team lost 9-7, but thanks to his once-in-a-lifetime performance, they almost scored one of the greatest upsets in fencing history.

The Soviet quartet went on to win the Olympic Team gold medal in 1960 and 1964, while Zhdanovich and Sisikin took the individual gold and silver in 1960. When I spoke to Dad about this near-monumental upset, his eyes widened as he responded, "All I could think about on that day was how incredible it would have been for two Jewish boys (he and Albert Axelrod, who won the other three bouts) from City College to beat the Soviet machine."

In 1960, Danny made his fourth consecutive trip to the Olympics in Rome, where the US team tied for fourth and took fifth.

In 1961, although he was out of shape and leaning toward retirement at the age of forty-four, Danny put an exclamation point on his legendary career. At the Martini & Rossi International Competition held at the New York Athletic Club, he scored a monumental victory over twenty-two-year-old French Champion and future World Champion, Jean-Claude Magnan.

In addition to Magnan, Dad's competitive career included wins over Olympic Champions Zhdanovich (1960), Egon Franke (1964) and Witold Woyda (1972) and World Champions Allan Jay and Eduardo Mangiarotti. According to his coach, the late Rene Pinchart, Dad was able to succeed against the absolute best in the world because of "his indescribable sense of distance."

The late Csaba Elthes, the five-time US Olympic Team coach and longtime coach of Olympic bronze medalist Albert Axelrod, was adamant that "Danny Bukantz was the greatest American foilist, definitely."

And although he could have made the Olympic Team in 1964, his competitive fire had burned out. It was the dawn of a new stage of his fencing career, this time as a referee, a position that was at that time called a "director."

* * *

Danny was selected as the American referee to the 1964 Tokyo Olympics, the 1968 Mexico City Olympics, the 1972 Munich Olympics, and the 1976 Montreal Olympics. Along the way, he officiated the finals in all three weapons (foil, saber, and epee). He developed a reputation of unsurpassed competence, consistency, and integrity. Danny had an easy-going personality that drew people toward him, no matter the language barriers. He didn't have a single enemy in the fencing community because there was simply nothing to dislike about Danny Bukantz.

Chaba Pallaghy, who was Chair of the International Fencing Federation's Referees Commission from 1992-96, once said, "Dr. Bukantz's acceptance and recognition, when fencing was totally dominated by Europeans at an elevated level, by inviting him to referee at the most important event, the Olympic Games, is extraordinary in itself."

After his string of eight Olympic visits was broken in 1980, thanks to Jimmy Carter's idiotic Moscow boycott, Danny's ninth Olympic Games appropriately took place in the United States at the 1984 Los Angeles Games.

For Los Angeles, Danny was chosen to be a member of the Directoire Technique, the small group that runs the competition and acts as Head Referee. And the Los Angeles Olympics were special for another reason: they were a family affair as I also participated as a referee.

In 1985 we shared another great father-son moment when we were both invited to referee at the NCAA Championships. Actually, we inadvertently caused a bit of a ruckus there. The jackets we wore as referees at the LA Games were a gaudy canary yellow. They were so hideous that there was no way either one of us was ever going to wear them in public, let alone in the privacy of our own homes.

However, as a means of adding a little class to the NCAA event – a little tongue-in-cheek class I suppose – we decided to wear the ugly Olympic jackets. It wasn't meant to show anyone up; it was just in good fun.

Well, the NCAA officials didn't see the humor. The jackets had the 1984 Los Angeles Olympics patch on their breast pockets. You see, the NCAA is quite anal about that kind of stuff, right down to the minutiae. Their rules don't allow athletes, coaches, or officials to advertise any product, company, or organization.

And heaven forbid! We broke the rules. So, thanks to the Bukantz boys, a new rule was crafted starting the very next year and is still in effect today (I know, as I'm currently the Head NCAA Referee): all referees must wear a blue blazer and at the event they are given a circular NCAA patch to wear on their breast pocket.

In 1987 Dad and Mom flew to Phoenix to watch me compete in the Nationals, which was the final qualifying event for the Pan American Games Team, basically the Olympic Team equivalent of the year. The way things shook out, the competition came down to a single bout, only I wasn't in it.

At the time, Greg Massialas and I were mortal enemies. Massialas was to face Pat Gerard in the final eight, but he was already on the Pan Am Team. He was in a position to keep me off the team by dumping the bout to Gerard, who would then in effect leapfrog over me. Massialas had the power to make sure I didn't attend the Pan Am Games that year as a competitor. Dad and I were very concerned that Massialas might do just that.

So, in a joking manner, Dad went up to Massialas before his bout and offered him a bottle of scotch if he won. Well, he did! I'm sure we both got drunk that night... although definitely not together.

Thanks, Dad!

3

Mexico City and Munich

I was only eleven in 1968, but that was the year I got my first taste of the Olympic Games. Dad received his second Olympic refereeing nod and brought my mom, Alice, and me to Mexico City with him. While he spent his days inside the fencing arena, I was trading pins with others old and young. At eleven, I wanted to be anywhere but at the fencing competitions.

Mom dressed me in a schoolboy blue blazer and let me loose so that I could trade pins either at the Villa Coapa, the newly built housing project for Olympic officials, or in the Olympic Village.

The Olympic Village? You may be wondering how I found my way into the Village. Well, back in 1968, it was extremely easy. My dad received a "D" identity card, as did all Olympic officials. Evidently, with the right connections (ours was George Worth, the Olympic Fencing Team Manager and former Olympic teammate of Dad's), spouses of officials were able to get the "D" identity cards as well. That identity

card enabled the holder to get into any venue and sit in the
VIP seats without a ticket. My mom, an extremely resourceful
person, went to one of those old photo booths with me and
had a passport-size photo taken of the two of us. She then
ripped her own photo from her identity card and glued the
new photo of both of us in its place! Yes, in 1968, it was as easy
as that. So, we were able to attend any and every event at the
Mexico City Games. Hey, I was only eleven, so hanging out
with my mom was still somewhat acceptable!

At the end of the day I'd come back to the room and
both of my lapels would be covered with the most exotic pins.
For an eleven-year-old, I knew how to drive a hard bargain
(although I'm sure I was taken to the pin cleaners along the
way!). Come to think of it, George Worth, who had a famous
collection of Olympic pins, cherry-picked my most valuable
ones. But, what the heck, the "D" identity card he got for
Mom was worth its weight in gold in Mexico City.

Thus, my most vivid memories about Mexico City – my
first Olympic Games! – had nothing to with fencing at all.
What I do remember, unfortunately, was coming down with a
serious case of Montezuma's Revenge. For those of you lucky
enough to have never experienced it, Montezuma's Revenge is
a terrible virus that non-Mexicans get when they drink non-
purified water or eat food that has been washed with non-
purified water. To put it kindly, I had it coming out of both
ends at the same time while running a nasty temperature. It
was a nightmare that only got worse when I tried to sleep to get
out of my misery.

Mom and I stayed in the same room, a room infested
with killer mosquitoes that dive-bombed us all night long.
Mom's solution was to turn on the lights and start whacking
at the mosquitoes on the ceiling with the heels of her shoes.
Of course, when she did that, the ceiling, which was made
of stucco, started crumbling on our heads! *Viva Mexico?*
Phooey!

Another classic non-fencing moment occurred in the cafeteria. The three of us ordered hamburgers, probably because they were the safest thing on the menu. One hamburger cost twelve pesos. When we went to pay, the cashier told us that we owed him forty pesos. Dad, incredulously, asked how that could be, but the cashier wouldn't budge; he insisted that one hamburger was twelve pesos, two hamburgers were twenty-four pesos, and three hamburgers totaled forty. Dad argued, got nowhere with the cashier, and decided that the four-peso rip off would be worth its weight in storytelling.

So, between throwing up, constant diarrhea, killer mosquitoes, stucco raining on my head, and hamburger surcharges, I don't remember much about the fencing I was forced to watch in Mexico City.

But there is one fencing memory that I do have, and, unfortunately, it's not a pleasant one.

Dad was a referee during the women's individual foil finals. As one of the most respected and highly trusted referees in the world, he generally received assignments in the final rounds of all the major competitions. So this level of high-profile refereeing was old hat for Danny Bukantz. What happened next was something no one expected.

In one bout, a Soviet fencer named Galina Gorokhova was performing an illegal tactic: she was covering her target with her unarmed back arm.

The fencer's target area in foil is basically the torso. A foil fencer's arms and head are not target areas. If you score a hit on the arms or head, it's considered "off target," the equivalent of the fencing foul ball. If a fencer puts his or her back (non-fencing) arm in front of his or her torso, the fencer is illegally covering valid target area.

Some fencers do this as a tactic to reduce their valid target area. Whether intentional or not, the move is strictly prohibited. Because referees watch the two fencers while their blades move as fast as one hundred miles an hour, it's not always easy to see if illegal covering is taking place. For that reason, arm judges are often used specifically to identify such transgressions.

There are referees out there who choose to take the path of least resistance and "look the other way" when it comes to fencers covering target or committing any infraction. Making the right call is guaranteed to incur the wrath of the fencer and the fencer's coach, which is the reason so many referees chicken out.

But Dad rightfully penalized Gorokhova for her offense. And then the politics of the fencing community reared their ugly head; Dad was not only overruled after a protest, but he was actually removed from his position in the middle of the bout.

In his critically acclaimed book *By the Sword*, (Random House, 2002) author Richard Cohen wrote the following about Gorokhova: "Gorokhova was also well known for her backhand parry. Even her teammates looked askance at this – 'she fences with two hands,' they'd joke sourly – but her coach was a high-ranking KGB officer with wide-ranging influence within fencing, so she was inviolate."

Another story Cohen detailed was how and why Gorokhova was disqualified from the 1971 World Championships by referee Guido Malacarne (who, twelve years later, would fail me in my international referee exam) for cheating by favoring her opponent, Anna Pascu of Romania.

This fencer clearly did not have a sterling reputation for honesty.

I sat there in the stands and couldn't believe what I was seeing. How could they do that to my dad? I wondered. How could they have the confidence to assign him to the Olympic finals and then humiliate him like that? How could this happen when everyone in the arena saw the Soviet fencer blatantly commit the offense repeatedly?

Well, let's just say that there are "valid answers" to those questions. In the fencing community, as in all walks of life, politics always come into play. And, in this case, political pressure from the Soviets evidently rendered my father the sacrificial lamb.

The moment was tragic; my heart was broken. Even though I was so young, I knew that the moment was a terrible one for Dad. And, looking back, I'd like to think I vowed to never let something that unjust happen to me, but the reality is that I had no idea I'd ever find myself in the position.

Maybe, just maybe, the first small seeds of admiration were planted that afternoon. Those seeds started me on the course that would become my goal in life: I wanted to follow in Danny Bukantz's footsteps. At the ripe age of eleven, I wanted to avenge the wrongdoing he suffered in Mexico City. I was ready for a fight, but I wasn't expecting such a battle.

* * *

Four years after the upsetting ending at the Mexico City Games, Dad was selected to referee at the 1972 Olympics in Munich. Including the four Olympics that Dad competed in, this would be his seventh straight Games!

My parents decided that I would once again attend the Games, but by this time I was a wide-eyed fifteen-year-old. Because of the timing of our Munich trip, I would have to miss the second month of summer camp – my absolute favorite time of the year. Looking back, I guess the trade-off was worth it: a trip to the Olympics was priceless (and this was definitely before MasterCard had coined the term!). I wasn't able to drive a car yet, but I'd been to two Olympics.

In Mexico City, Mom had taken care of me, but the family game plan was significantly different for Munich. Mom is a Holocaust survivor and had no interest whatsoever in setting foot in Germany that year or ever again. She decided to take a trip to Israel, appropriately enough, to visit relatives there. Dad and I planned to meet Mom on the French Riviera for a relaxing end to the dual trips.

In Mom's place would be my cousin Keith Raphael. This was great news to me, of course, because it meant that instead of the inevitable arguments I would have had with my mother, I'd have someone to enjoy the Games and bond with. What I didn't take into account was how different Keith and I had become. Though we were only separated in age by a year and a half, we were worlds apart. I, apparently, was an immature fifteen-year-old from the city, and Keith was advanced – in as many ways a sixteen-and-a-half-year-old country boy from New Britain, Connecticut could possibly be!

As an aside, the month at Camp Woodcliff that July was terrible. I was interested in sports, sports, and, well, sports. The others in my age group were interested in girls, girls, and smoking pot. Let's just say that cousin Keith would have had one amazing summer at Camp Woodcliff.

But we both ended up in Munich, where my interest in sports would finally be rewarded.

After arriving in the city, the three boys moved into an apartment. While Dad had his refereeing responsibilities to attend to, Keith and I were basically on our own for two weeks. We decided to go to as many events as possible (and figured out how to score tickets later). And, although there weren't any "D" identity cards floating around like there were in Mexico City, you have to keep in mind that the Olympics in '72 were substantially more relaxed than they are now in many ways – mainly, more tickets, much less security. At the time, Keith and I were running all over Munich looking to get our hands on whatever tickets we could find; we had no idea the Olympics were about to change forever.

Tickets for most of the events were still available. If we couldn't get a pair at the venue, we'd take a short train ride to the "official" ticket black-market – the giant square named *Marianplatz.*

In the days leading up to the Opening Ceremonies, we often went to the fencing practice facility. That was where we bonded with the great American fencers Carl Borack and Marty Davis. We met the Israeli fencing coach, Andrei Spitzer, as well.

One day after practice, I innocently asked Borack, "Hey Carl, do you think Keith and I could hitch a ride with you guys back to the Olympic Village?"

"No problem," he responded.

We got on the fencing team's bus, and as we approached the Village checkpoint, I distinctly remember ducking down behind late Princeton Coach Stan Sieja. The guard took a glancing look at the bus from outside the window and matter-of-factly waved us through. Think about that for a moment! Do you think that would ever happen during an Olympic Games nowadays? No one thought twice about how easy it would be to sneak any person (with any motive) into the Olympic Village.

Between meeting other legendary athletes, rubbing elbows with some of the best in the world, and nearly having our eyeballs pop out of their sockets while watching the beautiful women athletes, Keith and I were satisfied customers of our Olympic Village venture. (Yes, even for me that summer, sports finally took a backseat to gorgeous women!)

There was something indescribable about hobnobbing with these larger-than-life superstars. They all carried an air of something I was getting my first taste of, something that would make a huge impact on my life forever: *patriotism*. It appeared to me that these athletes were not only proud to be in the competitions, they were also proud to represent their countries. It wasn't about good versus evil; it was about national pride, plain and simple.

Later in the week we saw the US men's basketball team defeat Senegal in an early pool round. Little did either Keith or I know that later in the Games some blatantly biased and/or completely incompetent referees would give the Soviet Union team a tainted gold medal victory against the US. It was such an egregious insult to the US team that, to this day, they have never accepted the silver medals awarded to them. Those medals are still housed in a vault in Lausanne by the International Olympic Committee.

Keith and I watched some field hockey, and afterward decided that was the most boring event of all. We saw swimming and diving and plenty of track and field. We attended the fencing events, hung out in the Village challenging all comers at ping-pong, and spent some time with members of the US team. And, yes, under the supervision of my father, we forayed into some of the famous Munich *brauhauses* (beer halls). Hey! It was absolutely legal over there.

One day, Dad came up to us and said he had access to a block of tickets for the Closing Ceremonies. Evidently, the Cuban fencers were selling theirs at face value, a hundred marks (about $30 at the time), in order to pocket the American dollars. In my mind, the definition of a fair deal is when both sides are happy. While the American dollars undoubtedly meant more for the quality of life for these lucky Cubans when they returned home, Keith and I knew we could sell the tickets at Marianplatz and make a considerable profit.

So we took the first couple tickets and went to the "official" scalping zone of Munich for a test run. We learned the German words for "Closing Ceremonies" (*Schlussfeier)* and "one" through "five," and went into black market action.

The first few tickets sold for three hundred marks – ninety bucks! – a neat and tidy profit for a mere few minutes of work. Forget the other sports, scalping quickly became our favorite Olympic event.

We zoomed back to the fencing hall and gave Dad the green light to purchase every single ticket the Cubans had. In no time, Keith and I had fistfuls of tickets to the Closing Ceremonies, the last event of the Games and the hottest ticket around. We soon became very familiar faces at Marianplatz.

As we got a better handle on the market, our tickets soon

went for five hundred marks – $150! It was sick! It was a game that we were winning; the profit was almost incidental. In a perverse way, Keith and I had become Olympic participants.

Well, all good things must come to an end, and the *Schlussfeier* scalping did when we were nailed by the Munich Polizei. They confiscated the pair of tickets we tried to sell them, took our names down ("Yes, sir, my name is David Greenspan…"), and we headed for safer ground at the fencing venue.

It was at this venue that my life would change forever.

The stirring I began to feel in Mexico City would become a full-blown desire.

Most fans root for an athlete; I rooted for a referee. It was nerve-wracking to watch Dad refereeing down on the strip because he was constantly in the line of fire. He had a reputation for being one of the most honest and competent referees in the world (judged by his past performances as a referee during the '64 and '68 Games), a reputation that could have become severely tarnished after a single bad call out of the thousands a ref makes during a competition. But it never had, and it never would… even after the politically motivated incident in Mexico City.

From my vantage point, he appeared to get through all the bouts just fine. The only thing left to the imagination was what the coaches were screaming at him in their native tongues. (I never thought, for a single second, that I would eventually find out…)

As I watched those bouts, something inside of me changed, both in my view of the sport and in my view of life.

In the summer of 1972, I officially caught the fencing bug.

Of course, during the two weeks I was in Munich I had experienced many great things. I thought being inside the Olympic Village was cool. I thought scalping the tickets at Marianplatz was cool. I thought just being there at the Olympics was cool.

Then it hit me: actually participating in the Olympic Games would be the coolest thing of all.

It was in Munich that I decided to go for it. But I didn't know what I was getting myself into. I didn't realize what a tortuous journey I was about to embark on. I didn't have a clue about the pressure and sacrifice I would encounter as a result of this decision. What scared me most was that I didn't actually know if I could accomplish the ultimate goal.

However, I did know that my newfound enjoyment of fencing coupled with the love I felt for my dad would lead me down a path that would forever change my life.

Once Dad finished his refereeing duties (and there were no more Cuban Closing Ceremonies tickets to scalp), we hopped a plane to Nice a few days before the official end of the Games. As planned, the three of us would join Mom, who would be flying in from Israel.

We met at the hotel in Juan-Les-Pins, on the coast north of Cannes. That night at dinner we all planned to catch up; everyone had stories to tell.

After requesting a change of table at least once, one of Mom's prerequisites for adding tension to the dining experience, we finally settled into the restaurant's atmosphere for a feast of French cuisine. The waiter came around with menus and asked us, quite matter-of-factly, if we had heard about what had happened in Munich. No, we definitely hadn't! It was our waiter who broke the horrifying news of the terrorist attack that had occurred. We were shocked. We were sickened. We were absolutely speechless.

For crying out loud! We had been in Munich that morning! How could this have happened? Were the Americans safe? How about my friends on the fencing team?

After finally digesting the information, which was the only thing digested during that sorrowful meal, we all became very angry. Why would anyone do such a thing? Who were these animals? What would happen now?

Would the athletes be freed? Would the Games continue? Would the situation worsen? How many athletes had been killed already? How would Israel respond? How would the world respond?

The whole situation seemed so surreal. Despite being in Munich that morning, we all seemed so removed from what was happening. It just didn't seem possible that this could happen or that it would happen. We were just all so numb.

Reality hit home when we found out that Andrei Spitzer, the Israeli fencing coach, had been murdered along with ten other Jewish athletes. Keith and I had just met him only a few days earlier, and now that friendly young man was gone.

There was an incredible twist of irony to the horrible tragedy. Mom had accompanied Dad on two previous Games in Rome and Mexico City, but would not, under any circumstances, set foot in the country responsible for the Holocaust.

While living an upper class life in Czechoslovakia with her parents, Malvina and Julius, and her siblings, Clara and Robert, the Germans invaded and uprooted the family in one fell swoop. They were taken to a concentration camp, and, on the first day, the five were separated. Just like in the movies, the parents were sent in one direction and the children in another. The family shared a hug and cried, not knowing what their futures would bring. It was the last time Alice, Clara, and Robert would ever see their parents again.

Malvina and Julius Ellenbogen were murdered in the gas chambers.

Somehow, the three children were able to survive. Mom recognized early on in her eleven-month imprisonment that their best chance for survival would be to volunteer for every and any job or chore at the camp.

After they were liberated, the remaining Ellenbogens were able to board a ship to the United States. They landed in Boston and soon traveled to New York to join their Uncle

Martin Ellenbogen, who had been in America since before the war.

One of my mother's cousins, Judith, decided to start her new life not in America with her sisters Anne and Vera, but rather in Israel. In the summer of 1972, Mom went to visit Judith in Israel for the first time.

Black September was a rude reawakening for all of us. It was a reality check, one that hit us right between the eyes. The events reminded us of who we were and the anti-Semitism we would always face. It further illustrated that Israel would always be a target for hatred.

At the age of twenty, my mother's life was turned upside-down during the Holocaust. At the age of fifteen, the Munich Massacre left an impact on me, albeit not anywhere near that of what she went through. Munich would serve to crystallize my views of the world and accept that some will never "get it." No matter what personal beliefs anyone could possess, there was nothing that Israel or its athletes and coaches had ever done to deserve what happened.

But you wouldn't know that if you listened to some in the mainstream media. Long after Munich, the late Peter Jennings even rewrote history in defense of the terrorists. Disgracefully, Steven Spielberg's movie *Munich* goes so far as to suggest that Israel's subsequent response of systematically killing those terrorists was somehow a wrongdoing equivalent to the terrorists' murder of the eleven innocent Israelis! How dare he! I guess too much time in Hollywood has corrupted Spielberg's moral compass.

Simply put, 1972 was a summer I'll never forget. It was a summer of extreme highs and a single, heart-wrenching low. It was the summer I officially caught the fencing bug – and that is a moment that has stayed with me forever.

4

Stumbling into Dad's Footsteps

So, between catching the fencing bug at the Munich Olympics and starting my competitive career in high school, the lightning bolt hit me, and I decided to dive into fencing.

Make no mistake about this: I wanted to fence. I wanted to compete. I wanted to succeed in the sport. But, first and foremost, I wanted to follow in Danny Bukantz's footsteps. No matter how I look back at that time in my life, everything led directly to those feelings.

I loved my dad. I was so proud of my dad. I wanted to be just like my dad, especially when it came to fencing. And, so, the lifelong journey began.

Dad was a National Champion and an Olympian. And, naturally, those were the goals I set for myself.

While every fencer dreams of attaining those lofty goals, only a few have the added incentive and pressure of wanting to duplicate the success of a parent at the same time. Yes, this new challenge I had brought upon myself provided a healthy dose of motivation topped with an unhealthy dose of stress. Reaching for those special goals was one thing; actually attaining them was a whole different ball of wax.

Once a year a champion is crowned. In order to win a national championship, everything must fall perfectly.

Once every four years an Olympic Team is selected. In order to earn one of those coveted spots, everything must fall perfectly.

There is never a guarantee that those who have the most talent or who work the hardest will get to either of those pinnacles. Of course, without talent and effort, there's no chance at all.

Dad was a thoroughbred fencer. Within a few years of picking up his first foil, he was already a top contender. In short order, while at the City College of New York, he won the Intercollegiate Fencing Championship, the precursor to the NCAA Championship.

After graduating from college, he was already an Olympic contender. If not for World War II and the subsequent cancellation of the Olympic Games in 1940 and 1944, my dad could have competed in six Olympic Games.

Fencing came easily to him; he was a superstar right from the start.

Despite the hope that pedigree would propel me immediately to the top, it never happened. I didn't click with fencing the way my dad did. I was a natural athlete in many sports, but when it came to fencing, I was a plodder.

While my dad won the National Collegiate Championship only a few years after starting to fence, I couldn't even *qualify* for the New York City High School Individual Championships! In fact, I was only the fourth best fencer my junior year and the second best on my senior team. I had quite an inauspicious entrée into the sport.

After a few initial setbacks, roadblocks, upsets – whatever – it hit me that following in my dad's footsteps might not be so easy after all. And with that extremely depressing thought,

I decided to use my adverse experiences as a mantra for never giving up.

I have always been a fighter, a spirit I received from my mom. So, while I don't mention Mom much when it comes to this journey, there is no doubt that the single biggest attribute I possess – the will to succeed – comes directly from her.

It became clear that there had been some generation-skipping in the Bukantz talent department. All I had inherited from my dad, apparently, was his sizable nose and butt. But I was the sum of both of my parents, and there's a certain beauty to Mom's strongest attribute – her indefatigable will – that kept me going. Believe me, I needed every ounce of that will to keep trying, as the early failures continued.

I did have some early successes, however. I won some low-level competitions and earned the lowest rating possible of "C."

While I managed adequately against my fellow low-level peers, I also ventured into the highest level of competition against the wishes of dear old Dad. He correctly reasoned (although I didn't see it that way at the time…) that I was not nearly ready for that jump. He was of the opinion that I would likely be destroyed by seasoned fencers and develop a "loser's" mentality. Well, what teenager ever listened to his parents? I didn't and I paid a hefty price: the loss of confidence from early thrashings. It took a few years to regain it.

Dad was always very supportive, though I think he was dying inside watching his only son fail to become a top fencer. The years went by, I continued to train, and I never stopped believing that the dream would come true.

Without this perseverance, the quest would have met a terrible death. I would have quit fencing very early on in my career.

Instead, I maintained that C ranking, the lowest one possible, from 1975 until 1979. I just couldn't make the jump to a B, and the ultimate A rating seemed far out of reach. But I decided to keep on trying and always believed I would one day get that A rating.

One of the big problems in the early years was my weight. I ballooned up to two hundred and fifty-pounds in late 1975. Obviously, my weight was something holding me back.

5

Readjusting the Bar and the Scale

I was in a no-win situation. Actually, I put myself into that position; I wanted to be an Olympian and a National Champion, just like Dad.

Was it a realistic goal? Not really.

Was the bar set too high? Probably.

Did I honestly believe that I could attain both – or even either! – of these lofty goals? Well, yes… and no.

At the outset of my career, these goals were merely pipe dreams. I struggled for a few years, and those dreams seemed completely out of reach. But, by the spring of 1977, as I was just starting to emerge as a competitor, I had a life-changing, spur-of-the-moment conversation that allowed me to readjust the bar and set a more realistic goal.

I was walking to the subway one night after practicing at the NYFC, which was then located on the second floor of the Lancaster Hotel on the corner of Madison Avenue and 38th Street. As I left the NYFC for the 42nd Street subway station, a fellow fencer, Tibi Friedman, joined me.

Tibi was bursting with excitement because he had just clinched a spot on the United States team for the World Maccabiah Games, which would take place in Israel that July. I asked him how he had qualified and he told me he earned points at the National Championships. The top three Jewish fencers in each weapon (foil, epee, and saber) would capture a spot on the US Maccabiah Team.

As of that evening in 1977, I had never before even *qualified* for the US Nationals. The Metropolitan Section, of which I was a part, had the deepest field and was naturally the most difficult section to qualify from. In order to earn a spot on the Maccabiah Team I would first have to become one of the top twenty-four fencers in the country so that I could enter the closed point events. In order to make the top twenty-four, I first had to earn substantial points at the US Nationals. That was the only way to crack into the closed point events, in which I'd have to earn enough points to become one of the top three Jewish foil fencers in the country.

I was optimistic; I knew I was already a better fencer than Tibi Friedman.

I'm not putting him down here; Tibi was experienced, wily, and able. But, even with whatever lack of self-confidence and self-esteem I had at the time, I still knew I was better than Tibi. I regularly beat him in local competitions and usually placed higher, too.

So it was then and there that I made my decision. Somewhere on 38th between Madison and Sixth, I truly believed that I could earn a spot on an international team. It wasn't the Olympic dream; perhaps that bar was set too high. On that night, I set my sights on the US World Maccabiah Team, in effect readjusting the bar I had set five years ago in Munich to a more reasonable and – hopefully – preliminary, height.

Or so I thought.

Dad competed in the third Maccabiah Games in 1950, so I was, in effect, still going after my initial goal of following in his footsteps. But he didn't just compete; he won the gold medal in the foil event. So of course, while making the team was well within my reach, I decided I'd also have to win the gold medal at the Maccabiah Games.

Oy vey! What was I getting myself into? The bar I thought I was lowering now again seemed untouchable. Making the team was one thing; winning the whole damn tournament would be an entirely different ballgame. I found myself in a quandary. Nothing meant more to me than duplicating Dad's fencing feats. Only his feats were all so impressive! How would my "feats" ever be big enough – impressive enough – to fill his gigantic footsteps?

He wasn't just a good fencer; he won *four National Championships!*

He wasn't just a National Champion; he was a *four-time Olympian!*

He wasn't just a great referee; he refereed the *finals of the Olympics!*

He didn't just make the US Maccabiah Team; he *won the gold medal!*

I had to accept the reality that if I wanted to follow in the footsteps of Danny Bukantz, I would have to shoot for the stars. Anything less than the ultimate goal would render me a failure.

So, I went into this with the knowledge that I was likely to be a 'failure.' Nice choice, Jeff!

I must stress that Dad, from the very beginning, understood my untenable position and consistently assured me that he would love me no matter how things turned out. He told me, "Make your own name. Make your own friends. Appreciate whatever level of success you attain."

It meant so much to hear those words. But, while his heartfelt words of wisdom didn't fall on deaf ears, they couldn't deter me. I loved my dad, and I was going to spend as long as it took to be like him, at least in the fencing world.

That walk to the subway with Tibi gave me the courage to go for it. And I did – with a vengeance. I started training like a madman. I had the confidence and drive to go after a spot on the US Maccabiah Team – at the very least.

In order to make the tough climb up the national point ladder, I had to really put my nose to the grindstone. As a friend once joked about my sizable nose, "Bukantz, I'd love to see the size of that grindstone!"

But, there was a rude awakening when I didn't even qualify for the US Nationals… again… in 1977. Although I was good enough to qualify from any section in the country, I just kept falling short in the loaded Metropolitan Section.

I was so depressed that I fasted for nearly a month! I survived on Velamints and small containers of juice. I was a physical and emotional wreck. I stopped training – without the Nationals on the horizon, there was nothing to train for. I went to sleep at 6 p.m. nearly every night that June.

I just counted the days until I would make my way up to Camp Scatico in Elizaville, New York. Up there, I could forget about fencing and failure, and just enjoy the eight weeks of happiness and fun that was waiting in my mind-clearing Shangri-La.

As I approached the front gate to Camp Scatico, the depression was replaced with goose bumps and excitement. The camping experience was a weird hybrid of fantasyland and stark reality, as non-stop fun was always just a heartbeat away from potential disaster. As current Director of Scatico David Fleischner likes to say, "Camp is basically two months of near misses."

After the head start from my June swoon of fasting, I was driven to lose a ton of weight that summer. I disciplined myself to eat healthy foods and run every day on the ball field with my buddy Ben Krull. Maybe I was just tired of failing.

While the heavy weight on my shoulders to succeed would always be there, I could control the extra weight under my shoulders.

I was the Division Leader for a group of about twenty teenage boys. While acting as these kids' parent for two months was challenging, it allowed me to recharge my batteries, which had been eroded by the yearlong pressures of fencing.

For those lucky enough to go to summer camp, you know what a tremendous life experience it provides. As a camper, you are basically on your own to fend for yourself, deal with others, and overcome adversity. As a counselor, you also get a sneak preview of what it is to have the responsibility of a parent.

Basically, camp offers two months of life lessons, and regardless of your age, you return home a lot older and wiser.

But, there is another aspect of camp that cannot be underestimated. You are allowed to be a completely different person from who you were at home or at school. In other words, the nerd can become cool, the loser a winner, the outcast a popular kid. You come to camp with a clean slate, and you have the opportunity to let your persona evolve.

I was never a cool kid. Instead of getting into the drug scene, I preferred to play sports. I was a natural at tennis, baseball, basketball, and hockey. (In fact, I made the Forest Hills High School tennis team. Thankfully, my sport of choice was fencing; had I stayed with tennis, let's just say that my kids wouldn't have any footsteps to worry about.)

While 'cool' will never describe me, at least at Camp Scatico I was able to be a little more popular than at home. The kids loved me, my peers respected me, and for a few summers I was one of the bigger men on campus.

Even though I was a Division Leader, I was also the part-time fencing counselor. As far as anyone at Camp Scatico knew, I was the best fencer on Planet Earth. Heck, they didn't know that 'Buk,' as I was known, couldn't even qualify for the Nationals.

So, even though my confidence was in the basement, at least the campers thought I was the man. As I said, you can be someone different at summer camp.

One day, my group was scheduled to have inter-camp games. Another camp would bring the same-aged kids, and they would compete in a few different sports during the day. It was usually a nice change of pace, and something the kids always looked forward to. After all, it was the chance to show them that Camp Scatico was the best.

As the visiting campers and counselors arrived on the campus, I immediately recognized one of the counselors as fencer Leonid Dervbinskiy. Dervbinskiy had come over from the Soviet Union a few years earlier and was a top epee fencer. In fact, he had won the US National Epee Championship in Portland, Oregon one month earlier.

So, after we embraced, the kids demanded that one event be added to the day's inter-camp schedule: A bout between Dervbinskiy and Buk.

Imagine that; the last thing I wanted to do in the summer of 1977 was fence. I hadn't picked up a foil since May, when I failed to qualify for the Nationals. Dervbinskiy, on the other hand, was in tip-top fencing shape and raring to go.

So the big bout was set: Leonid Dervbinskiy, the National Champion, versus Camp Scatico's favorite fencer – who couldn't even qualify for the Nationals! – the ever-popular 'Buk.'

As only foils were available, we fenced foil. This was to my advantage. But it didn't matter. While there were no electrical lights as proof, or a referee to make the calls, it became glaringly obvious to the untrained eyes of the campers who was the man in this bout. Dervbinskiy pretty much dominated me.

And just like that, the veneer was destroyed. Not only was it demoralizing for the Scatico campers to see their hero beaten, but no longer was 'Buk' even considered the best fencer they had known.

Thankfully, the kids still loved me for who I was, even though my fencing persona, of all things, was destroyed. It was akin to the Wizard of Oz being unmasked when the curtain was opened by Dorothy.

I hated fencing more than ever on that fateful day in July, 1977.

But I learned that summer that my life would not be solely defined by wins and losses on the fencing strip, but rather by character displayed and respect earned.

Any doubts that I had lost my peer's respect were erased at the conclusion of the summer during team selection for the Color War, the grand finale of the camp season. The camp is divided into two teams, Green and Grey, which compete for four days, by age group, in all of the usual sports. Counselors who display the greatest leadership skills are selected as Generals for the two teams. For the second consecutive summer, I was selected by my peers. Let's just say that vote of confidence made me forget about not qualifying for the 1977 Nationals and the embarrassment of the Dervbinskiy duel.

It was a summer of extreme highs and lows. I arrived at Scatico that summer weighing two hundred and thirty-two-pounds, depressed, and with virtually no self-esteem. By the time I returned to Forest Hills, I was a new man. The loss of fifty-two-pounds led to a huge gain in morale and self-confidence.

The change in mindset and work ethic paid off. When I arrived home from camp in late August and tried on my only suit, the size 42 pants fell directly to the floor without touching my once-gigantic hips.

I was a new man. The weight loss was directly proportional to a huge gain of confidence. I felt so good about myself that I became very comfortable with girls and had great success in the dating game. It was amazing how the weight had been holding me back in so many aspects of my life. Even more amazing was how I started to grow as a man – and a fencer – when I shrunk to the size of a normal person.

During the year that followed my dramatic weight loss, my fencing naturally improved. A huge part of the rapid improvement was because I was lighter. An even bigger part of my newfound success was due to the self-confidence I had never before possessed.

My progress was steady, not meteoric. I harbored thoughts that maybe fencing success wasn't really meant to be, as I still couldn't improve upon that damn C rating. But, as the saying goes, "All things come to those who wait."

I got rid of the excess weight, but this *wait* was killing me! However, I was beginning to see the light at the end of the tunnel, and for the first time believed that the light wasn't coming at me from an oncoming train.

In 1978, I finally qualified for the US Nationals, which were held in Hallandale, Florida. I made a huge splash in my first national tournament. I breezed through the three preliminary rounds, which was no cakewalk, and made it into the quarterfinals, the money round where points were first awarded. Finally, I had made the point standings!

At that time, direct elimination wasn't used, as pools were employed throughout the competition. In the quarters, the top twenty-four fencers were seeded into four pools of six based on their results in the previous rounds. The top three fencers in each pool qualified for the semifinals. A fencer would generally need a record no worse than 3-2 in the pool to qualify for the next round.

My pool, due to bad luck of the draw, was the toughest of the four. I won my first two bouts against Olympian John Nonna and Peter (Ashley) Burchard. When this happened, there was a buzz around my strip – as a newcomer to the national scene was beating the big boys.

Although I continued my hot fencing, I lost three very close bouts to Olympians Mark Smith and Ed Donofrio, and Heik Hambarzumian. Those three, by the way, had all won National Championships.

I finished the pool with a 2-3 record and was eliminated. I tied for thirteenth place, but placed nineteenth after my indicator, or touch count (the differential between the touches I scored and the touches against me), was calculated. That relatively insignificant differential would prove significant to me.

As it turned out, my nineteenth-place finish put me twenty-fifth in the point standings. Had I scored two more touches in my pool, I would have been eighteenth in the competition and twenty-fourth in the national standings.

The closed national point events were still limited to the top twenty-four, which meant I wouldn't be eligible to compete in them during the 1978-79 season. After everything I had done at my first Nationals, **two touches** basically held me back for yet another year! Breaking into the point standings had proven to be one tough task. Missing my mark by the slimmest of margins on a tie-breaker was just too much to take.

I was distraught, to say the least. Two touches would render me as first alternate and keep me out of the loop for another whole year? You've got to be kidding me!

Based on the hurdles always in my way, I probably should have been a high-hurdler.

6

What a Difference a Year Makes

The summer of '78 was quite different than the previous year.

Camp Scatico was the same. The trials and tribulations were the same. The fun was the same. The practical jokes on the kids (and other counselors) were the same. The quasi-Utopian existence was the same.

So, what was so different?

It was my outlook. Whereas in 1977 I didn't want to think about fencing for one minute, in 1978 I couldn't stop thinking about it.

After all the years of would haves, could haves, and should haves, I had finally made my mark on the national scene. Danny Bukantz's son was on the move, and there was no stopping me now.

Usually, I hated to leave camp and return to the reality of the city… the real world. But in 1978, after my great result at the Nationals, I couldn't wait to get back to the Fencers Club.

There was one other difference that summer, as I met my eventual wife, Carol Irwin. As much as I couldn't wait to get back to fencing, I was really sad to leave her on the last day. Would it be a superficial summer romance? After all, Carol lived in Wilmington, Delaware, which seemed like a foreign country to this city boy. Well, regular Amtrak excursions commenced a week after camp ended, and we're still together.

As always, I went down to practice on opening night, the day after Labor Day. I was ready to make the next step. No longer would I have some type of pseudo-confidence, as I always (sort of) believed I could do it. Now, I had real confidence, because I had done it!

I had approached each season as a gambler approaches each new bet or night at the track. I used to go to the harness races, and each night brought with it a new chance to win. No matter what happened the last time, or the last race, each new one brought with it a new hope, a new chance.

In gambling, this was, of course, a delusional outlook. It was inevitable that any high hopes would be dashed and the gambler would leave a loser... again.

In fencing, however, I controlled my own destiny. And my destiny was to follow in my Dad's footsteps.

After just missing the semi-finals of the US Nationals, the top twelve in the country, my destiny was assured.

So I came into the 1978-79 season with a new outlook and a new confidence – and dove in headfirst. Actually, drove in headfirst!

I was working in Livingston, New Jersey as an investment broker. After work I'd get into my car and schlep into Manhattan at the peak of rush hour. The traffic was beyond brutal getting into and through the Lincoln Tunnel, but eventually I'd make my way up to the Fencers Club, which had moved to 71st and Broadway, where the "real" fun began. Of course, sometimes (well, every night) the "real" fun was delayed for another half hour as finding a parking space in the city proved to be a frustrating and daunting task.

I'd quickly change, stretch for ten or fifteen minutes, and race down from the locker room to start fencing. Practice sessions typically lasted between two and three hours, during which time I would take a lesson from my coaches Csaba Elthes and later Semyon Pinkhasov, and spar with my clubmates. The sparring was often contentious, as the winner of the bout stayed on the strip and took on the next person in line. The Fencers Club was usually crowded, so maintaining your position on one of the strips was key. Otherwise, you waited in line and wasted valuable practice time. Because of this, some of my clubmates fought extra hard to win the self-refereed bouts and constantly argued over who scored a touch.

My philosophy when sparring was not so much to win, but rather to practice certain moves. Unlike others in the club who only concerned themselves with winning and staying on the strip, I knew better. I knew they were only fooling themselves when they claimed touches were theirs when they were actually mine. Here's an area where my experience as a referee helped me immeasurably. When we went to competitions, where the refereeing was objective, my clubmates were in for rude awakenings when the refs were making correct calls.

There was a pecking order at the Fencers Club. There were elite fencers – the top dogs. Then there were the next-in-lines, the up-and-comers, who were pretty good fencers. After these were the old-timers and lesser-fencers, also known as "cannon fodder." And there was no avoiding the fact that you'd have to wade through all three levels over the course of an evening. This certainly wasn't the optimal use of training time, and, on some nights, the elites would stay at the club even later in order to procure their own strip and have a concentration of strong bouts.

For the few of us shooting to make international teams, let's just say that mind games were rampant. In fact, I started to detest a couple of my teammates due to the unnecessary evil of it all. I wasn't able to become good friends with some of them until we were done competing against one another. I didn't even invite some of these teammates to my wedding in 1982. The training sessions were long. They were grueling. And since fencing is done with steel swords, I regularly walked away from practice with all sorts of abrasions and scrapes. My oh my! Did they ever sting when taking a shower! After the shower, I'd dress and make my way to the car. Practice always left me sweating profusely, which continued even after drying off. So by the time I walked to my car, my clothes would be drenched – again! But no matter how spent I felt after practice, I always had a good vibe going after that workout.

It usually took forty-five minutes to an hour to get back home to New Jersey. Even at that time at night – around nine or ten – there was the inevitable traffic jam getting out of the city via the Lincoln Tunnel. Sometimes I had to drive farther south into the city and try the Holland Tunnel. Most times I'd sit in traffic and start punching the steering wheel.

By the time I arrived home, it was usually already 10:30 p.m., sometimes even later than that. And then, totally exhausted, I'd sit down to eat dinner.

This was the routine three or four times a week – sometimes five! – from Labor Day until the Nationals in June the following year.

And on the weekends there was no rest for the weary. Saturdays and Sundays were when the real action took place in the way of competitions. I probably fenced three weekends out of every month. Fencing quickly became my second full-time job; I was beginning to feel like a hamster running in place on a wheel.

There were monthly open tournaments in New York City, at which all of the top fencers in the Northeast would compete. These were basically mini-national events, as the level of competition was fierce, and while they didn't count for national points, personal pride was always at stake. There was an omnipresent "King of the Hill" attitude among the top fencers, and winning a New York Open was a big deal.

In addition, many top fencers traveled to New Jersey for open events. Whereas New Jersey Opens used to be relatively weak and totally insignificant, that all changed with our "Keep up with the Joneses" mentality. No one wanted to miss a competition and give someone else a leg up on bragging rights. Subsequently, the New Jersey Opens became New York Opens west of the Hudson.

While the New York and New Jersey events were the local staples, I also traveled to non-point events such as the Cornell Open in Ithaca, New York and the Cherry Blossom Open in Fairfax, Virginia.

I'll never forget that first Cornell Open; it was my first competition outside of the New York City area. After an emergency pit stop in the men's room, I arrived on the strip for my first bout of the day against Greg Massialas, who was already one of the top-ranked fencers in the country. As if my opponent wasn't enough of a problem, I apparently was so nervous and oblivious that I forgot to zip up my fencing knickers. I was undressed before and during that bout!

And – as if all of these tournaments weren't enough – I was also invited (read: "required") to participate in Olympic Training sessions held every month in New Jersey.

But it was total dedication to my new goal and the sport itself that pushed me past the obstacles. I was in great shape; the former two hundred and fifty-pound slob was now down to an athletic 185. At the Olympic Training sessions, I had the second *lowest* percentage of body fat behind Peter Westbrook. My butt had shrunk down so much that Mom actually asked me in her syncopated Slovak accent, "Jeffrey, darling, does it hurt to sit down?"

The combination of practicing and competing against the top fencers in the region finally gave me the confidence in myself that I once lacked. Now I knew I could beat anyone in the country. I no longer felt as if I was merely cannon fodder. I was a threat.

I was somewhat of an "idle threat," though, as I still couldn't compete in the closed national point events. Having been relegated to first alternate (*ugh*!), I basically became known as the best fencer in the country *not* eligible to enter the closed point events.

I qualified for the 1979 Nationals, slated for June in Colorado Springs, and I was ready. I was ready to better the previous year's 19th place finish. I was more than ready to earn my way into those just-out-of-reach closed point events. I was ready to follow in Dad's footsteps. I was ready to make the next jump.

I approached the Colorado Nationals with a will to win, as opposed to a fear of losing. My head was in the right place. I was in great shape. I had a nice taste of success in Florida in 1978, but I was hungry for more... a lot more.

On the day before the individual competition, my FC clubmates Jack Tichacek, Michael McCahey, John Nonna, and I took a car trip to the summit of Pike's Peak. I always loved puns and couldn't resist telling the guys, "I hope we didn't 'peak' a day too early." That beauty was received with the usual array of groans and laughter.

The next day, unfortunately, was no laughing matter for me, as I was eliminated in the third preliminary round and didn't earn any points. It wasn't my day, no excuses. It was a long flight home and an even longer summer of discontent.

Was I destined to be a fencer who would never make the big time? I was starting to have those thoughts, those self-doubts.

All summer I wondered which result was the fluke: The great 1978 Nationals or the crash and burn 1979 Nationals?

The summer of 1977 had me hating fencing. The summer of 1978 had me loving fencing. And the summer of 1979, my last at Camp Scatico, had me confused, and once again doubting my ability to follow in Dad's footsteps.

The Turning
Point

After returning home from camp in August 1979, I was in the best shape of my life. I had continued to run daily and spent the summer playing basketball on the counselor team. Carol and I continued our relationship, which had blossomed during the, shall we say, 'off-season.'

Oh, to be a camp counselor again… While I hated to leave the fantasy world of Camp Scatico, this time for good, I just couldn't wait to start fencing on opening night, the day after Labor Day.

I arrived at the Fencers Club with a certain swagger that night. I was ready to make the jump… again. I was ready to duel until the death to reach the elite level. I was tired of waiting. I was tired of false starts.

Yup, I was the gambler going to the track one more time with the hope that no matter how many times I had lost, this would be the one!

I trained hard that season, going down to the club about four times a week. I was in shape, I was driven, and I was finally confident... again. I set my sights on the first "Open" foil competition of the season, which would be held in late September.

Amazingly, after being the quintessential patsy and also-ran, I won the competition! Winning the tournament meant I finally improved my C rating, and due to the strength of the tournament, I jumped right past the B rating and earned the highest rating of A!

So, at the age of twenty-two, an age at which many of today's fencers mull retirement, I had finally made it as an elite fencer.

I was an A! I did it, and nobody would ever be able to take that accomplishment away from me. I was so happy and so proud. After all the dark times – after all the devastating losses and fear of failure – I was finally able to make my dad proud too.

Of course, his happiness and pride only then surfaced in my eyes. As he had told me so many times, he was just so proud of me for giving the sport a try and sticking with it. In his eyes, I was never the failure I always thought I was in my own eyes.

Now that I had a taste of success, there was nothing that could stop me from wanting to taste it again. There is no question that the unexpected victory supplied the mental boost I had needed. As Yogi Berra said, "90 percent of the game is half mental."

I won the next Open, thereby maintaining the once-elusive A. In fact, I won a whopping four Opens in the Metropolitan Division during the 1979-80 season, which earned me the #1 ranking in the division for the season. Considering my past performance chart, it was an incredible feat. I had to pinch myself to make sure it was all really happening to me. It had come to be, in a surreal twist, that I was disappointed whenever I failed to win a competition.

I went from the loser's mindset that I developed when

I competed above my level (against my dad's wishes) to a winner's mindset. It took four years of blood, sweat, and tears, but it was definitely worth it.

My confidence was growing in leaps and bounds. While the Opens were pretty tough competitions, the proof would be in the pudding at the national events. Until I succeeded at that level, I would still have doubts about my emergence as an elite fencer.

But as it turned out, the turning point in my career happened at anything but a national tournament.

At the third New York Open of that tremendous '79-80 season, I encountered a really scary situation in the preliminary pool. I was slated to fence Ed Wright, a member of the 1976 US Olympic Team. Wright wasn't just an imposing figure because of his Olympian status; he was even more imposing as an individual. He was built like a fullback, lightning fast, and extremely belligerent.

Wright was intimidating to his opponents and referees – basically anyone in the room. My dad – calm, cool, collected Danny Bukantz – once had a horrible experience officiating for Wright at a National Championship.

I have to admit that even I was a little fearful of Wright. I didn't like him one bit. So a bout against him would be a tough task for many reasons, not the least of which was that he was an Olympian.

Our bout was heated right out of the gate. While I was not yet the official "John McEnroe of Fencing," I damn well wasn't going to cower to that bully – even if I was still in the infancy of my career. The battle escalated when Wright continued fencing after referee Carlie Coates' command of "Halt!" and forcefully hit me when I'd already let my guard down.

The after-the-halt hit didn't hurt, but it was completely against the spirit of the game. And, it happened to be against the rules! In fencing, you don't hit a defenseless opponent – ever.

I decided to chalk it up as something unfortunate that happened in the heat of battle. However, on the subsequent action, Wright did it again. He intentionally hit me after the halt a second time. Instinctively, I thrust my foil right back at him, while he was still facing me. I know, it was wrong, but it was a knee-jerk reaction in a combat sport.

I turned around and walked back to my en garde line (where fencers prepare for the next action) when I was blindsided by what felt like a bullwhip across my back. Wright had once again revealed his true colors. Not only did he continue to instigate the unsportsmanlike conduct, but he hit me… **from behind**… as hard as he could with his steel fencing foil.

Let me be honest. It hurt like hell! But, before I had a chance to respond, let alone comprehend what had happened, Wright loudly threatened, "If you ever hit me after the halt again, I will break your nose!" (Yeah, that's the PG version. In reality, Wright peppered the comment with some quite colorful language…)

The referee, Coates, was a meek guy to begin with; all he did in reaction to what was going on in front of him was stand there, still and silent. The original after-the-halt offenses should have warranted warnings for both of us, but Wright's full-force wallop to my back with his foil should have immediately expelled him from the competition. He should have also received supplemental discipline from the Metropolitan Division.

His verbal threat to break my schnoz should have warranted the same.

But Coates did nothing. He looked stunned and refused to sanction Wright despite my vociferous and incredulous protests. Incredibly, he decided to recommence the bout.

I lost the bout to that thug, but was sure I would win the war when the Metropolitan Division reviewed the incident and suspended him.

Unfortunately, the person running the competition, Ruby Watson, chose to submit a false report. Watson, who wasn't even in the room when the entire brouhaha occurred, wrote a report to the Metropolitan Division that basically denied any wrongdoing on Wright's behalf and indicated that I was the protagonist of the incident.

What actually happened was black and white, but Watson's report was skewed. Like Wright, Watson was revealing her true colors through the ill-fated report.

The end result, believe it or not, was that I was put on probation by the Metropolitan Division for my actions, while Wright was completely exonerated of any and all wrongdoing.

I wanted to kill them both! How dare Wright do what he did! How dare Watson lie about it! I was at wit's end. I was demoralized, frustrated, and in total disbelief of the outcome.

Leave it to Dad to advise: "The only way you can right this wrong is by beating Wright on the strip."

Easier said than done, Dad.

A few months later I caught wind of a competition in Tampa, Florida that was going to be televised on the local Public Broadcasting Station, WEDU. It was an annual event called the Gasparilla Open and it coincided with the annual Gasparilla pirate festival in Tampa. As fencing was rarely, if ever, on television, I decided to make the trip. The location was also convenient; Dad's older brother and his wife, my Uncle Sam and Aunt Jewell, lived there. So the whole family packed the weekend bags for the Gasparilla event.

As luck or fate would have it, Wright, of all people, also flew down to Tampa for the competition! So, while I really wasn't completely confident that I could beat him on the strip, and I still wanted to beat him senseless off the strip, there was a possibility that I could get my revenge, albeit twelve-thousand miles from the crime.

I breezed through the preliminary rounds and the direct elimination bouts. In the round of eight I beat a local guy.

In the round of four I beat Wright's New York crony, Ron Mason. There were no fireworks with Mason because – unlike Wright – he was an honest and decent competitor.

To get the gold medal, my opponent would be Wright. On television, no less.

Yes, the same Wright who hit me from behind as hard as he could.

Yes, the same Wright who verbally threatened to break my nose.

Yes, the same Wright who was the beneficiary of Watson's false report.

Yes, the same Ed Wright, 1976 Olympian, who I wanted to take out.

Well, this bout was shaping up to be a dandy. The entire time we dueled I just kept thinking about my dad's advice. I wanted to extract my ultimate revenge by beating Wright in this televised bout.

The score went back and forth as we inched closer to the magical tenth touch. Along the way there were late hits by both of us, plenty of yelling in the other's face whenever one of us scored a touch, and even some gamesmanship.

Wright found a dead spot on my *lamé* (the electric jacket that registers touches, pronounced "lah-may") in the neck area. That area corrodes the quickest due to sweat, but it is also covered by the bib of the fencing mask. Wright was simply trying to get my goat.

The referee, Jim Campoli, had no choice but to make me change into my back-up lamé. When I returned to the strip, I asked Campoli if I could test Wright's jacket as well. I went right for a green spot on the neckline and, wouldn't you know, I found a dead spot on my very first try. Wright sneered and I looked like the cat that had just eaten the canary.

Take that, thug boy!

We both worked over Campoli on nearly every call and he was clearly becoming agitated. But this bout was a virtual duel to the death because we hated each other.

In that WEDU studio, you could cut the tension with a knife.

The bout was tied at eight apiece. The next touch would be the dramatic turning point. One of us would be one touch away from victory, the other a touch away from defeat. At a moment like this, I knew I had to play the percentages. I had to win or lose with my best action. Yes, I had to rely on "Ol' Faithful," the counter-four riposte.

I knew Wright would attack, as was his M.O. I knew he would try to disengage around my initial four parry. I knew he would try to push me to the end of the strip. I knew he would come at me like a bat out of hell.

So I was ready for what was about to happen. The question was whether I could keep the correct distance and execute my bread and butter action.

We returned to our en garde lines and Campoli asked if we were both ready to begin again. "Ready," we both replied. "Fence!" Campoli instructed.

In an instant, Wright came at me at one hundred miles an hour. I retreated as fast as I could, just far enough to keep Wright out of my distance but not too far to keep me out of his if I parried his inevitable thrust. Wright feinted into my four line and expected me to bite by parrying into the four line. I did. Wright then disengaged under my blade and lunged at full force with his phenomenally long lunge at my chest.

The last time Wright went to hit me with this amount of force was when my back was turned. I certainly didn't expect it then, nor could I have been ready to defend myself against his dastardly act.

But, this time I was facing him, and was ready for exactly what came next.

In a flash, I instinctively executed my counter-four parry. I caught Wright's blade dead to right in a bear-trap with my blade. He was toast.

All I had to do was hit him with the riposte, but Wright was wily and quick. He tried to retreat out of distance. I needed to literally go the extra yard to reach him.

Whereas Wright's lunge was one of the longest in the country, mine was one of the shortest. So, in a blink I fleched, a flying type of footwork faster and more surprising than a lunge. The fleche went much farther than my lunge would have and I hit him square in the stomach.

I yelled in his face, jumped up in the air, and went to get ready for the next and hopefully winning touch. We went back to our en garde lines. Campoli commanded us to "Fence!" Almost immediately, the timekeeper yelled "Time!"

Yes! The time had run out. Yes! I was the winner, 9-8. Yes! I'd gotten my revenge against that creep.

And I'd done it Dad's way.

I jumped high into the air. Wright extended his hand for the customary handshake. Yeah, right, Wright.

As I came down from my jump for joy, I just slapped Wright's hand as hard as I could and ran off the strip and into the outstretched arms of my dad.

Recently, Bernie McGovern, the announcer of the match had this to say about that fateful day: "That was the perfect television bout. Apart from the personal animus and drama, you were at your colorful best and Wright was the ideal foil (no pun intended). That bout was actually instrumental in PBS deciding to run the Gasparilla on the network the next three seasons."

On that February day in 1980 in a Tampa television studio, I not only exorcized the demons of Ed Wright, but by beating an Olympian I exorcized the remaining demons of my self-doubts.

8

Farewell, Closed Point Events...Hello National Results!

In my breakthrough 1979-1980 season, the hits just kept on coming. The United States Fencing Association (USFA) replaced the unfairly restrictive closed points events for the top twenty-four fencers with something new. There would now be four point events, called the North American Circuit (NAC), and, best of all, these would be open to *everyone*!

Finally!

The local tournaments, Olympic training sessions, and the endless practicing at the Fencers Club were all important for one reason now: to earn points at the NACs!

At the NACs, the top twenty-four earned points. In any given tournament, there were generally 100 to 140 fencers entered in my foil events. In order to earn points, a fencer usually had to qualify through three or four rounds of pools, which were comprised of six or seven fencers and held in a round-robin fashion. The top half of the pool usually qualified, and that meant compiling a winning record in order to have a fighting chance.

The competitions were long and grueling. They usually started early in the morning and ended late in the evening. In the pools I fenced between seventeen and twenty-four bouts, depending on whether there were three or four rounds. In direct elimination I fenced anywhere from two to eight bouts, depending on how far I went into the tournament. Those fencers in the best physical shape had a distinct advantage at the latest stages of the finals.

The top thirty-two would be seeded into direct elimination (DE) bracket. In order to reach the top twenty-four, and earn those precious points, a fencer would have to win at least one DE bout.

On the new circuit during the 1979-80 season, I did well and made the finals in the last two NACs. I was climbing the ladder and finished the season ranked somewhere in the mid-teens.

I always believed I could crack the upper echelon. All I needed was a break, and the opening of the point events proved to be a gigantic break in my career.

My momentum continued at the first NAC of the 1980-81 season. This was the longest day of my fencing career and, at the time, my greatest. It was the Michel Alaux NAC held at Hunter College in Manhattan. Alaux, by the way, was my first coach. He died tragically of lung cancer in 1974.

The competition started promptly at 8 a.m. I reached the gold medal bout that night; actually I reached it the next morning, as the bout – and the competition itself – finally ended at 2:15 a.m.! As I was completely dehydrated, I couldn't leave doping control until 3:30 a.m.!

However, in order to reach the gold medal bout, I had to overcome a very tough teammate, Jack Tichacek, in the semis. Jack had been on the National Team for a few years and was already one of the top guys in the country. Not only that, but I was still a bit psyched out against Jack. We first fenced against each other in 1976 at the Junior Olympics (under-20 championships) in Troy, Michigan. At that time, Jack was so much better than me that I didn't honestly expect to have a chance.

Sure enough, in that 1976 bout Jack scored the first two touches in rapid fashion. At that point, I decided to try to let time run out and lose 2-0, because that score would have been better for my pool indicators (touches scored minus touches received ratio). Basically, I was employing the fencing equivalent of North Carolina basketball Coach Dean Smith's "four-corners offense." However, Tichacek smelled blood in the water and didn't plan on settling for a 2-0 victory when a 5-0 victory seemed on the horizon for his indicator.

So, he came right after me, broke through my ill-applied (but not ill-advised) four-corners defense, and wiped me off the strip, 5-0.

Well, a lot of time had passed between February 1976 and this snowy December night in 1980. Now, the question was whether I could overcome Tichacek both on the strip and in my head.

The bout started around 1:30 a.m. and we were both exhausted. Not only were we tired, but we both began to cramp badly. My left quadriceps were cramping and – worse – so was my fencing hand. My hand was involuntarily clamping shut on the foil, and then the cramp went up into my forearm.

The result of the cramping and exhaustion was that we fenced a very tentative and defensive bout. Basically, we were trying to keep the score close, and neither was trying to score the requisite ten touches. Instead, we were rolling the dice that time would run out with one of us in the lead.

This led to a tied score of 3-3 at the end of regulation time. The next touch would win. It was sudden death. I felt that Jack wouldn't expect me to attack, especially after sitting back for the entire bout. So, in direct contrast to my mantra, which is to go with your best action on a deciding touch, I decided to try a surprise tactic.

I attacked the surprised Tichacek with my last burst of energy. It worked, which probably surprised me, as well.

I'd come full circle since our first bout in 1976, where I was trying to lose by "only" 2-0.

Jack was one of the toughest fencers I ever faced. Beating him was not easy. Overcoming my initial fear of him was a lot harder.

I hit a full body cramp in the gold medal bout, which started after 2 a.m. Both of my quads gave out, and I fell over, face first, like a giant tree. My opponent, the great Mike Marx, looked down at me, shook my hand, and said, "Nice match."

After this 2nd place finish at a NAC, for the first time I actually believed I could fill some of Dad's biggest footsteps.

*   *   *

I was finally on my way. I truly believed that the 1980-81 season would culminate with the quadrennial World Maccabiah Games in Israel. I was on a mission; I had an attitude that could not be stopped.

Whether it was the drive, the newfound confidence, or perhaps just the natural progression of an athlete, I arrived that season. I didn't just earn points at NACs; I started regularly making the finals. Reaching the finals (the top eight in a tournament) meant that Danny Bukantz's son had finally arrived – and with a bang!

At the end of the 1980-81 season I went from an also-ran to the sixth-ranked foil fencer in the United States. That ranking earned me a top spot on the 1981 Maccabiah Team! Not only that, it put me on the US World University Games Team going to Romania. Incredibly, I only missed the US World Championship Team by one spot.

Every member of that year's team sacrificed so much for a common reason: to make it onto one of the 1981 teams. It's what we all wanted. It's what kept teammates from becoming genuine, mutual friends. It's what pushed us to the brink of exhaustion.

And after just two seasons on the national circuit, I was right in the thick of it. I could taste it. What used to be something of a pipe dream, no matter how hard I tried to convince myself otherwise, was now coming to fruition. I was in some rarified air, as only a very few ever get close enough to qualify for a team.

Having reached the "readjusted bar" by qualifying for the 1981 Maccabiah Team, and actually jumped way over the bar by making the World University Games Team, I had no choice but to set my sights on the original bar – the Olympic Team.

It was healthy to set some preliminary and more reasonable goals; but now that I had a taste of success in the big leagues, I truly believed I could make the Olympic Team in 1984.

What had forever seemed like a long shot was now well within reach. After stalling for half a decade, my career finally got in gear. With the success on the strip came this additional pressure.

No matter how many of Dad's footsteps I filled, I'd feel like a failure if I didn't become a second generation Olympian.

And, in this endeavor, there would be no consolation prizes.

9

A Bridesmaid and a King

Making the 1984 US Olympic Team would be tough sledding, because the field was loaded with the top foilists vying for the precious five spots. It was virtually guaranteed that three of the five would go to Mike Marx, Greg Massialas, and Mark Smith. Those were the three most dominant players of that era and almost always placed in the top four at NACs and National Championships.

Basically, everyone else was fighting for the two remaining Olympic berths. It was guaranteed to be a dogfight.

In addition to the big three, there was also a significant threat in the form of the relative neophyte Peter Lewison of the Fencers Club, who had emerged in 1983 and vaulted right to the top of the point standings. As the season progressed, it became clear that Lewison would procure one of the two "open" spots on the team. Actually, in 1984, Lewison became the top American foil fencer when he finished the season ranked #1 and finished twelfth at the 1984 Olympics.

With Lewison's emergence, it now appeared as if only one Olympic spot was truly up for grabs.

The others in contention for the remaining spot were by no means chopped liver. My FC teammates Michael McCahey and Jack Tichacek made every final that year, and the two of them trained together with the same single goal in mind. They were in the best physical and mental state possible during the 1984 Olympic run.

George Nonomura, who eventually made the 1988 Olympic Team, and Pat Gerard were past members of the World Championship Team and made most of the finals. Former Olympian Ed Wright (and 1980 Gasparilla *silver* medalist) was also in the running.

My buddies from the NYAC, Jim Bonacorda and Ed McNamara, were right in the mix. Of the rest of the field, my good friend Don Blayney of San Francisco was the biggest threat.

I just named twelve fencers who were legitimately in the running for the 1984 Olympic foil team. Every one of them had represented the United States at a major international event, which meant that in any given year each had finished the season in the US top five.

It was a baker's dozen at that, because I was also in the mix. After all, I had finished both the 1981 and 1982 seasons ranked sixth. I'd competed at the 1981 World University Games, the 1981 World Maccabiah Games, and the 1983 World Championships.

There were many other good fencers around that season, who, despite being unlikely candidates for the Olympic Team, were always capable of upsetting one of the big boys.

Among this dangerous group were Eric Rosenberg, Dave Littell (who eventually made the 1988 Olympic Team), Ed Kaihatsu, Philippe Bennett, Peter Burchard, Pierre DesGeorges, Joe Biebel, Paul Schmidt, and Lew Siegel, all of whom had proven capable of reaching the finals of a national competition.

The ground rules were set and they were crystal clear. The 1983-84 season would consist of four NACs and the Nationals. At the end, each fencer would count the top three of four NAC results and the result in the Nationals. The top five fencers in this point system would become the 1984 Olympians.

Everyone was under an immense amount of pressure. The FC became a pressure-cooker as McCahey, Lewison, Tichacek, and I were realistic candidates for the top five spots. The mind games were rampant, and it would be fair to say that except for McCahey and Tichacek, none of us were friends in 1984.

No one wanted another person to get the upper hand in any aspect, whether it was during training or competition. The New York Opens and even the New Jersey Opens became even fiercer, as they provided the monthly proving grounds for the Metropolitan-area foilists. Local tournaments were appetizers primarily for bragging rights; the main courses were the NACs, as they provided the Olympic qualification points.

Not to ruin the end of this tale, but let me sum up my year in three words: I finished eighth.

I was in the running all season. However, my Olympic dream was derailed by three crucial losses. If I had only won all three – as I should have and could have – I probably would have made the team.

In December, 1983, at the first NAC in New York, I was eliminated in the last bout before the finals and placed ninth overall. In that bout, I was leading Canada's top fencer, Luc Rocheleau, 7-1 in a ten-touch match-up. At that point, my left hand cramped – badly.

I pulled out every stall tactic in my repertoire to try and stop the cramping, but to no avail. Basically, I couldn't grip the damn foil. The cramps shot up into my left forearm; I was a dead duck. I tried and I fought and I clawed, but against a fencer of Rocheleau's caliber, it was only a matter of time. It was impossible for me to score any more touches because I had no control over my weapon. As for trying to defend my target area, that wasn't any easier.

The once-commanding 7-1 lead dissipated into a 7-10 defeat. I was frustrated and walked off the strip in tears. A win guaranteeing a spot in the finals would have been a huge start to the Olympic race, but I had to settle for a respectable ninth-place finish. My record for the day was 15-4.

It was on to San Jose in January 1984 for the second NAC. Quite frankly, I don't remember much about the tournament, let alone how I was eliminated. But I finished a disappointing eighteenth despite going 11-4 on the day.

Without a final in the first two NACs, I found myself in a huge hole. I was in this huge hole against fencers who had already made at least one, even two finals. For the rest of the Olympic qualifying season I would be playing serious catch-up. There was no room for error.

The third NAC took place in March in Chicago. I started slowly in the pools, but really came alive in the direct elimination bouts to steamroll through Blayney, Gerard, and Littell to reach the final eight – finally!

I had karma on my side during the Blayney bout. After building a 9-5 lead, only one touch from victory, he started to mount a rally. When this happens, the pressure can quickly switch from the fencer who was one touch from elimination to the fencer hanging on for the last touch.

And, hang on I did, but just barely.

Blayney's momentum and the additional pressure temporarily caused me to fence tentatively. And just like that, the 9-5 lead evaporated into a very tenuous 9-8 lead. At this point, I decided to be aggressive and try to finish the bout before Blayney caught me. So I attacked. Blayney, also a lefty, parried me in the four line and I was dead.

Then, something happened that to this day my coach, Simon Pinkhasov, swears was divine intervention or something like it.

When Blayney made his riposte, the light went on the machine. But the single light was my light, indicating that somehow I hit him on the remise (second action) and he somehow missed the middle of my ample chest with his slam-dunk riposte.

In situations like this, I was always a cool customer. I knew that I had to shake Blayney's hand, unhook as quickly as possible, and get the hell off that strip. Otherwise, Blayney might decide to try to find out what had happened; if an electrical defect was found by the technician, that winning touch would have been annulled. So I bolted and the win was in the record books. How I scored that last touch we'll never know. Over twenty years later, Pinkhasov still kids me about it.

And in that first round of eight, my opponent was McCahey, who would be pumped up in front of his hometown fans, friends, and family. Not that he needed any additional incentive, but McCahey had his eyes on the first prize, which was a Leroy Neiman fencing lithograph.

I decided a warm-up bout with Lewison was just what I needed. Now, typical warming up is like batting practice: it doesn't count. In fact, most fencers use the time to, well, warm up, as opposed to going all out to score touches. This is how my warm ups usually went as well.

On that day, for whatever reason, Lewison and I decided to go toe to toe. We treated the ten-minute practice session as if it was for the World Championship. It was a meaningless and nonsensical display of testosterone. But I was on fire and able to hit Lewison at will. Though it didn't count for anything tangible, it gave me a huge boost of confidence for my heavyweight match-up with my FC teammate McCahey. I needed that boost because of all the fencers in the country, McCahey was the one who had my number.

The bout against McCahey started how the warm-up against Lewison had ended. I built a commanding 7-3 lead, but then something happened. I couldn't score a touch. McCahey started a comeback and his entourage screamed louder and louder with each ensuing touch. It sounded like the Notre Dame (his alma mater) fight song was blasting from the loudspeaker.

I changed my glove, I changed my foil; I wanted to change my underwear! I was trying to stall, break his momentum – anything.

Alas, nothing worked. McCahey, destined for the 1984 Olympic Team (he would later win the National Championship, again in Chicago), scored seven touches in a row to win 10-7. After the bout ended I turned and dropkicked my mask for a long field goal across the gym. Luckily, the referee didn't see my outburst or I would have been black-carded and lost all of my points.

I finished eighth overall and had a 12-7 record in Chicago.

So, going into the fourth and final NAC in April, I had ninth and eighth place finishes to my name. The competition was the Cherry Blossom, held in Fairfax, Virginia. As in Chicago, I was on my game. I made the final of eight after beating Greg Massiaslas for the second time that day, this in direct elimination, which no doubt sent him straight to the hotel bar. I don't remember who I fenced and lost to in the finals, but I finished sixth with a record of 16-7 on that day.

Dropping my worst result in the NACs (the eighteenth place in San Jose), I still had an outside shot using my ninth, eighth, and sixth place finishes. In order to have any chance of making the Olympic Team, I had to place first or second at the Nationals in June back in Chicago.

The reality is that had I won the bouts where I led Rocheleau 7-1 and McCahey 7-3, I'd have gone into the Nationals just having to make the final eight for an Olympic berth.

But before the Nationals there were two huge local fencing competitions. The first was a New York Open, the last one of the season. I had won the first Open of the season way back in September, but that seemed like an eternity ago. I went on to win this final Open with a record of 14-2, ending the "Open" season as I has started it.

While the Opens are "open" to all competitors, the next competition wouldn't be so welcoming. The last event of the season prior to Nationals was the vaunted Tournament of Kings.

The Tournament of Kings was only open to those fencers who possessed the highest rating of A. It was the ultimate test, as every bout became a main event of sorts. And, adding to the degree of difficulty, the competition was a complete round-robin of grueling ten-touch bouts. In other words, everyone fenced everyone, and there would be no luck of the draw.

Nine fencers entered the tournament, which meant each of us would have eight bouts. I was on a roll that day, handily beating Maurice Kamhi, Demetrios Valsamis, Paul Schmidt, Lew Siegel, and Dave Littell. While those guys weren't exactly cannon fodder, I still had to go through fellow FC clubmates and Olympic hopefuls Lewison, Tichacek, and McCahey.

McCahey continued his streak against me. Whether it was a stylistic or mental clash, I don't know. I don't think I beat him the entire season.

I had much better success against Tichacek, but he was one crafty competitor. He thrived on keeping the upper hand mentally over his opponents, whether it was during practice or during a tournament. I always arrived at the strip in ill humor, and the bout was, shall we say, spirited right from the get go.

Tichacek didn't seem to like the way I was fencing and made some wiseass crack about me trying so hard. I wasn't in the mood for his mind games, so I got right back in his face and said, "What do you want me to do, roll over and let you win? I'm trying to win, too!"

And I did. At the end of the bout we offered each other a limp fish handshake, sneered, and remained anything but friendly teammates for the rest of the day.

My last bout was against the best fencer of the tournament thus far, Lewison, who was undefeated. If I won, only Lewison and I would have a single loss, which meant we would fence-off a second time for the gold medal.

Our first bout was like our "warm up" before the Chicago NAC. I continued my red-hot fencing to beat Lewison and force the fence-off.

Beating Lewison once in 1984 was a tall order, but beating him twice in a row would be unprecedented. We went back and forth until the score was 8-8. Then I scored two surprise touches to accomplish the improbable, beating Lewison twice in a row to earn the crown of King.

Going into the Nationals, I was peaking. I'd just won back-to-back competitions in New York, including the Tournament of Kings. If I could keep the winning streak going on my second visit to Chicago, there was still a glimmer of hope.

The pressure on everyone to do well in the Nationals was evident, especially on Tichacek, who only had to make the finals to gain a spot on the Olympic Team. Sadly, he lost consecutive bouts to Ed Wright and George Nonomura by 10-9 and just missed the finals and the team.

I had my work cut out for me, as I had to take a first or second place finish. I fenced very well, but ultimately came up short. In my final elimination bout, I again let one go that I should have won, losing to Joe Biebel 10-8.

The stars were not aligned that day, and despite a 15-4 record, I finished in a disappointing thirteenth place.

My four results from the three NACs and the Nationals (ninth, eighth, sixth, and thirteenth) were close, but definitely no cigar. In the 1984 Olympic season, my record in the NACs and Nationals was 69-26, a seventy-three percent win-loss ratio. I had nothing to be ashamed about. I trained hard, fought hard, and did my best. Unfortunately, I lost three devastating bouts during that long year. Had I won them all, my dream may have come true.

When I look back at the gut-wrenching year of 1984, I take solace that while I was an Olympic bridesmaid, I was also King for a day. If nothing else, that Tournament of Kings victory validated, once again, that I was capable of beating the best fencers in the country. It erased the last of my own self-doubts.

10

The World Maccabiah Games

The Maccabiah Games are held in Israel every four years, always a year after a summer Olympic Games. They are open to any country, but only to Jewish athletes. There's a popular joke about the world's shortest book: *Famous Jewish Athletes*; however, the reality is that there have been many great Jewish athletes. Ever heard of Olympic gold medalists Mark Spitz, Lenny Krayzelburg, Mitch Gaylord, or Sarah Hughes?

What separates the Maccabiah Games from the Olympics and other international competitions? The Olympics are basically a one-dimensional sporting event. The Maccabiah Games are lush with a unique blend of athletics, culture, and heritage. At the Olympics, athletes are housed according to nationality: Americans with Americans, Germans with Germans, Italians with Italians, and so on. At the Maccabiah Games, athletes are housed according to their sport, which enables the athletes to meet and mingle with their competitors from different corners of the globe.

The walk on 38th Street with Tibi Friedman back in 1977 game me something realistic (at the time) to dream about, and the dream was about to come true. What a feeling! I didn't think I could feel any higher until I got on the plane at JFK with four hundred other Maccabiah athletes for the chartered flight to Israel in July of 1981. Mine was a natural high from having made the team. But, the thought of actually competing for the gold medal, Dad's gold medal, had yet to cross my mind.

The teams from more than fifty countries marched into Ramat Gan Stadium for the Opening Ceremonies in front of 55,000 friendly fans. I was on cloud nine as I waved to the crowd while my heart swelled with pride. Proud to have made the team. Proud to be an American. Proud to be a Jew. Proud to have finally followed in Dad's footsteps.

Then it struck me: This lap around the track in Israel was one of the rare and special moments in my life when I, as a Jew, knew *everyone* was on my side.

As the foil competition approached, the nerves began creeping up on me. Now I know that all athletes get a case of nerves before a competition – it's completely natural. Mine were unnatural, however; I was focused not just on doing well, but **winning** the whole damn thing.

Elite athletes always want to win; very few, however, are in the position of having to win in order to consider their performance a success. For that matter, how many athletes actually have to win in order to reach the goal of following in their father's footsteps?

Those damn footsteps... Those damn gigantic footsteps...

On competition day I was ready. I was hot. I was in the zone. I was going for the gold! After qualifying out of the preliminary pools, I made it into direct elimination round. After winning my bouts and cruising into the finals – the top eight – I drew a young Israeli named Itzhak Hatuel, the son of the Israeli national coach. Hatuel, also left-handed, was short, strong, and an explosively fast fencer. But I was smarter and completely destroyed him, 10-3.

For the semifinal round I drew another Israeli lefty, Shlomo Eyal. Already a world-class fencer, Eyal had achieved far better World Cup results than any American fencer. But that didn't scare me; I was on a mission to fulfill a family legacy.

The winner of the bout would go on to the gold medal bout. Eyal was a fiery fencer who tried to intimidate both the referee and me, which raised the level of tension to that of the Gasparilla bout with Wright. Of course, that only played into my hands, as I was the master of these intimidation tactics. The score stayed close; we fought for each touch, but Eyal outlasted me and won the bout, 10-7.

I was beaten, fair and square. I ran into a fencer who was far better than me, but had come very close to upsetting him. While it was a tremendous feeling to hang with a world-class fencer, it couldn't soften the blow of failing to win Dad's gold medal.

I still had to mentally prepare for the bronze medal bout against a Frenchman, Fabian Bukobza. After regrouping from the previous bout to lead 9-7 – just one touch away from earning a medal! – I let the bottom fall out. For some reason (maybe the Frenchman really wanted to win a medal, too), he scored the next four touches to eke out an 11-9 victory.

I was demoralized. Distraught. I was so out of it that I ran out of the gym and cried. To come halfway around the world in search of something and fail to get it, or even the consolation prize, well, let's just say that finishing fourth was the worst place for Danny Bukantz's son.

*   *   *

When an athlete or team doesn't win the tournament, the series, the bowl, etc., the mantra or battle cry is usually "Wait till next year!" But in the case of the Maccabiah Games, I would have to wait four years until my next shot at Dad's gold medal. A lot can happen in an athlete's career over a four-year span, but I was determined to earn a return trip to Israel in July of 1985.

As it turned out, I just missed the Olympic Team in 1984. I had done my best but others had done better. However, unlike my competitors, I actively refereed. It was a thrill to go to Los Angeles as an extra referee for the Summer Games. In fact, I did officiate the first round of the men's foil and performed well. While this was a great accomplishment, a footstep partially filled, it wasn't officiating the finals.

Danny Bukantz always refereed the finals.

I made the US Maccabiah Team in 1985. As a veteran, I knew what to expect, and I knew what I wanted to do. No matter how you cut it, anything less than the gold medal wouldn't do.

After cruising through the preliminary rounds and early direct elimination bouts, I once again reached the finals. As a stroke of incredibly bad luck, in the final of eight I drew my Fencers Club teammate and best friend, Eric Rosenberg. Yes – the same Eric Rosenberg from Cardozo High School who led that team's charge to beat "that fat ass son of Danny Bukantz."

Well, it was thirteen years later – a lifetime. We had become traveling buddies and great friends. On the fencing strip, however, there are no friends. Not in my world, at least, not with the legacy I was chasing.

Quite frankly, I was ranked much higher and had been considerably more successful than Rosenberg. But since we trained together every night, we knew each other's game inside and out. This is always a huge advantage to the lower-ranked fencer, as it evens out the playing field to some extent.

We were both very tense during the bout and fenced accordingly. On one action, Rosenberg unintentionally brought his forearm up into my mask and really jolted me. Such physicality only added to the tense atmosphere.

When this happened, the score was even, 3-3. On the very next action, Rosenberg again reacted instinctively and unintentionally during an infighting action by clobbering me under the chin with a flailing forearm smash. In the heat of battle, I immediately punched him on the back in retaliation. His actions were physically irresponsible, but my response was unacceptable. But consecutive jolts to my chin – I literally saw stars! – that's just how I reacted.

As mentioned previously, I am never phased when things get a little crazy on the strip. But my good friend (well, he didn't think so for the rest of that trip!) Eric was thrown. He was so riled that he started attacking as fast as he could, which played into my hands, as his attacks were no match for my defensive game and calm demeanor.

After the punch, I scored the next seven touches in rapid fashion and won the bout 10-3. I had earned my return trip to the semifinals, the final four.

I again drew Hatuel, whom I beat easily at the 1981 Games. But by 1985, Hatuel had become Israel's top foil fencer. In fact, he had placed second at the toughest World Cup in Paris. He was a top international fencer and I was not. But I didn't care about rankings – I was chasing a legacy.

Hatuel and I battled evenly until the score reached 8-8. The next two calls by the referee brought "Boos!" from my teammates and tears to my eyes. The video replay showed both actions to be mine; however, the French referee Serge Plasterie didn't see it that way.

Here's the bottom line: the Israeli Fencing Federation brought in two international referees for the Games. These two refs received an all-expenses paid vacation at the Netanya seaside and didn't have to work all that hard as the competitions weren't that large.

I always believed that these refs felt somewhat sympathetic or indebted to their hosts and, in return, gave the Israelis more close calls than they deserved. For the two calls after the score reached 8-8, I will always wonder if this was the case. In my opinion, Plasterie was simply too good a referee to have blown both calls – they were simply crystal clear actions.

I made a beat attack – my best offensive move. It meant beating Hatuel's blade with a crisp movement of my blade, thereby giving me the right-of-way, the attack. Then I fleched, a move I was so proficient at that Rosenberg had named it "The Blaster." I was basically blasting my opponents with the power of the attack.

So I blasted. Hatuel counterattacked. Both lights went on. I jumped for joy and did a war whoop, having taken a 9-8 lead. But no! Plasterie, with slight hesitation, ruled that Hatuel had parried The Blaster and it was his riposte that had scored.

My teammates yelled and booed. We were all incredulous. The call had been wrong and the timing couldn't have been worse. Instead of being one touch away from the gold medal bout, I was now one touch away from my second Maccabiah bronze medal bout. That's one hell of a difference, to say the least.

And all because of a terrible call.

After arguing with Plasterie to no avail, I had to prepare for the next monumental touch. I calmed myself down, accepted the bad call, and decided to overcome it. That's what champions have to do. Losers plan their eventual excuse for the loss, but I was no loser. With Dad's gold medal at stake – and within reach – I had to get the next touch.

And I had to go with my best action. That's what Dad always told me to do. When it's down to the last touch, win or lose with *your* best action, not your opponent's!

There was no other option than to go with the counter-four parry riposte. That's the move that brought me to the dance, and I was leaving with it.

Hatuel attacked. He fell right into my trap. I caught his blade perfectly with the counter-four parry and riposted. He remised, basically left his point out after being parried, and both lights went on again as we both landed touches.

I had tied the score with my bread and butter move!

Or so I thought.

Unbelievably, Plasterie thought the opposite. He ruled that Hatuel had made the beat attack. Oh. My. God. I wanted to strangle that Frenchman! He screwed me – blatantly! – and he did it right in my face. He deprived me of the chance at winning Dad's gold medal.

Why did he do it? *How could he do it?* I was stunned. My teammates went nuts on him. He completely reversed the two calls, both of which were perfectly executed actions initiated by me. I went from winner to loser – just like that!

Sour grapes? You bet. Was I robbed? You bet. It was a travesty, but the match was over and I, once again, had to refocus for the consolation prize, the bronze medal. After the four-year wait, a very empty and frustrating four-year wait, I defeated the Israeli Haim Brahmi to win the Maccabiah bronze medal.

I was very happy that I hadn't finished fourth – again. I was even happier to have won a medal. But there's no denying that my happiness was diminished by having failed to win Dad's gold medal – again.

That year I also entered the individual epee competition. There was an open spot, I had fenced a little epee in my time, so I thought, "Why not?" I had nothing to lose. I actually purchased my two epees from Santelli Fencing Equipment the day before I left for Israel.

There is something to be said about competing with little or no pressure. I went into the epee event relaxed and loosey goosey. But, as a competitor, I still wanted to win. I certainly hated to lose. I did well in the preliminary pools and made it to direct elimination. I made my way to the finals and in the round of eight I drew the top Israeli epeeist at the time, whose name I've long since forgotten. But I'm sure he'll never forget mine.

Early in the bout, I hit him in the solar plexus with a stiff and hard thrust. It was not brutal; it appeared to be a run-of-the-mill touch. My opponent turned around to get ready for the next touch, went to his en garde line, and collapsed. Evidently, the ultra-stiff shot totally knocked the wind out of him. Only he wasn't getting up. The doctor on call was brought over and determined that the Israeli couldn't continue the bout. He was taken by ambulance to the hospital five minutes later. Jeff Bukantz: Winner by TKO!

In the papers the next day the Israeli press trashed me for having committed some heinous act. That wasn't the truth at all, as it was nothing out of the ordinary; my technique was perfectly legal. Hey – in my defense – fencing is a combat sport!

I dispensed of a very tough Canadian, Ron Bakonyi, in the round of four. Though Bakonyi was the #1 seed and his father/coach Peter, himself a world class fencer, was yelling and screaming on the sidelines, I somehow pulled it off.

Surprisingly, I earned a spot in a different gold medal bout! My epee success came out of nowhere. US teammate Arnold Messing, a cantankerous, crafty old-timer from Brooklyn would be my opponent. Messing had never won any popularity contests with me, the rest of the team, or the fencing community in general. We actually had to draw straws to determine who would get stuck with him as a roommate. (Dave Mandell drew that straw, by the way.) Messing just seemed to have a knack for sucking the oxygen and joy right out of a room.

I think this example is fairly representative of Messing's persona. There was a poster hanging in the locker room at the City College of New York (his alma mater, as well as Dad's) inscribed with Will Rogers' quotation, "*I never met a man I didn't like.*" Underneath, some anonymous detractor scrawled the following rejoinder: "*He never met Arnie Messing.*"

On that day my teammates really made their opinion of Messing known. They broke with customary etiquette and vociferously cheered for me in the gold medal bout. In a match between teammates, this is considered taboo. Not that time, though.

I'm still not sure if it was love for me or disdain for Messing, but the team really rallied around me. And I was on fire – no "Messing" around for me! It was a no-contest victory. I fed off of my teammates' support and blew him off the strip in a decisive 10-6 win.

Now, this was completely unexpected and I was understandably ecstatic. Holy cow! I won the World Maccabiah Games epee gold medal! But the medal wasn't earned in foil; it wasn't Dad's gold medal. Isn't that something? To win a gold medal and be disappointed because it was the "wrong" gold medal? Well, those were my honest emotions as I flew back to the States that July.

"Wait till next year!" Again!

*   *   *

Well, it was another four years before I got the chance to compete in another Maccabiah Games. During that period, my career continued to blossom. In 1987, I was ranked fifth in the country, which landed me a spot on the Pan American Games Team and World Championship Team. At the Pan Ams, held that year in Indianapolis, I earned a bronze medal in the team foil event. But the highlight of the Pan Ams was having my parents, my wife Carol, my great summer camp buddy Tommy Rosenberg and his wife Karen, and my eighteen-month-old daughter Stephanie in the stands, along with 80,000 countrymen cheering us on as the United States team marched into the Opening Ceremonies at the Indianapolis Speedway.

As luck would have it, I once again just missed the Olympic Team in 1988. I was incredibly disappointed – I even thought about retiring! Most fencers retire after an Olympic quadrennial ends. Most fencers aren't Danny Bukantz's son, with a legacy to fulfill. I decided to give it another year.

It was the 1989 Maccabiah gold medal, Dad's gold medal, or bust!

The 1988-89 season turned out to be my best ever. I ended the year as the second-ranked foil fencer in the country and earned my third berth on both the Maccabiah Team and World Championship Team. As they were held at the same time, I did the opposite of what most athletes would do; I passed up the far stronger and prestigious Worlds, which were being held in Denver, in order to have one last shot at fulfilling my dream. A grizzled veteran, I couldn't wait for what I prayed would be my date with destiny. It'd been twelve years since Tibi Friedman had made the team and told me about it on the way to the train. Twelve long years since I first believed I could make it as well. If I didn't win the gold this time around, I would have to settle for a lifetime of emptiness. Mine was not an envious position to be in.

But if, by chance, I could pull it off, all the years of insane pressure would be worth it. So off to Israel I went for my last gasp at getting Dad's Maccabiah gold in foil.

The Opening Ceremonies were held on the day before the foil competition. Under normal circumstances, I might have considered staying back in the room. Standing in the brutal Israeli heat for three hours before marching into the stadium would have been terribly draining the day before the biggest moment of my competitive life. However, these weren't normal circumstances, as I had the honor of being one of the athletes to carry a banner and lead the team into the stadium. So despite the heat, this was too cool to pass up.

On competition day I was more nervous than ever. I knew this would be my last shot. As the saying in competitive sports goes: "There will be no tomorrow."

As in 1981 and 1985, I qualified easily out of the preliminary pools and braced for the direct elimination draws. However, there was an unexpected, yet all-too-familiar roadblock waiting for me. Incredibly, for the second consecutive World Maccabiah Games, it was Eric Rosenberg. Amazing. Best friends fly halfway around the world and draw each other twice in a row – and in the knockout round at that! Even more unfortunate, for both of us, was that this direct elimination bout was just to reach the final eight!

And it only got worse. For whatever reason, I was flat during the bout and Rosenberg was hot. In the ten-touch bout, he surged to a huge 7-3 lead. After that seventh touch I turned around, walked to the end of the strip, stomped on a potted plant, and took off my mask. I had to buy some time and try to figure out how to turn this around.

I loved Rosenberg as a friend and respected him as a fencer, but it would have killed me to lose such an important bout to him. I was better than Tibi Friedman; I was better than Eric Rosenberg. I just couldn't go out this way.

So I thought, "What would Dad say?" What would the legendary Danny Bukantz tell his son?

I thought about the time I came back from 0-4 to win 5-4. All I remembered was Dad's tongue-and-cheek reaction: "Schmuck, how did you let him get ahead 4-0 in the first place?"

I took a breath. And then I remembered the actual advice Dad would have given: "Keep your distance, Jeff!"

Yes! That was it! I was allowing Rosenberg to get a little too close. So, down 3-7, I opened the distance just enough to throw him off. I scored the next seven touches, just as in 1985. And we managed to stay friends afterward, as I didn't even have to punch him this time.

The comeback was monumental. But it only got me into the final eight. I still had to win three more bouts against tough fencers. In the round of eight I struggled to beat the sneaky Hungarian – I know, that's redundant! – Gabor Riesz, 10-6.

In the semifinals, the final four, I drew the young Israeli, Siegal, a model who had all the girls cheering for him... but not for long. I dispatched him rather quickly – 10-4, over and out.

Finally, after twelve years of hard work and determination, I reached the gold medal bout.

My opponent was another Israeli, Katz. He was half my size, half my age, and twice as fast. And in the beginning of the bout his speed got the best of me; he built a 7-5 lead. He was three touches away from turning my dream into a nightmare. Between touches I took off my mask and tried to concoct a tactic that would slow him down. Once again, I decided to alter the distance. Dad's harping on about keeping the distance always resonated with me.

This time I shortened the distance in an attempt to slow the Katz Express down. The key to overcoming his blinding speed was to keep the train from leaving the station. I stalked him and stayed very close. My hand speed could match his from this distance, while his foot speed would be neutralized.

I scored the next two touches to tie it up, 7-7. At this point, my teammates in the stands turned on the video camera. And I will be forever grateful for that. They started chanting. From the stands I heard a sing-songy "Buuu-kantz, Buuu-kantz." On the video, you can clearly hear Rosenberg saying, *"He's closing the distance."*

After all the years, the tears, and, yes, the fears, my dream was about to come true. Only one problem: the referee was again Frenchman Serge Plasterie. I worried that history may repeat itself.

In what seemed to be slow motion – like a dream sequence – I scored the next touch on a textbook riposte to take my first lead of the bout, 8-7. Then, having closed the distance, I surprised the young Katz with a slow attack to make it 9-7.

This was the moment I had waited for, trained for, prayed for, yet never really believed would arrive. Normally, after scoring a touch, I'd take off my mask, wipe the sweat from my face, and take a short breather. Not this time. After scoring that ninth touch, I tightened my mask, turned around, and immediately got back into the en garde position.

I had blown a 9-7 lead in 1981 for the bronze medal. That was the thought going through my mind. There comes a time when you have to let go of the past and have the guts to go for it – to grab the reins of the future. And I did.

Plasterie said, "Allez," (French for "Go"), and I once again surprised Katz by attacking. He counterattacked and both lights went on. Oh no! What would Plasterie call this time?

He pointed at me. Four years after breaking my heart with two horrible calls, Plasterie pointed at me and said, "Attack." It was my touch.

After the winning touch I jumped into the air in a spastic show of emotion and flipped my mask into the air. By the time I had landed, the video shows I was already crying uncontrollably. Finally! Tears of happiness. Tears of unbridled emotion that only a father and son could understand.

And, while I basked in the lofty air of a champion, I could just see Dad smiling all the way from Forest Hills.

Rosenberg immediately recognized the monumental family accomplishment and didn't waste one second before he made fun of my love for publicity. "Oh, look out!" he said. "Bukantz is gonna go to town with this. *West Essex Tribune*, here we come! West Essex Jewish Sports Hall of Fame, here we come!"

Obviously, there was no such hall.

It was July 4, 1989. I'll always remember the actual date because it was the night the entire US Maccabiah Team celebrated at the team gala. After the award ceremony, we called some taxis and zoomed over to the shindig in Herzliya. It was late and the evening was winding down, but not before the announcement was made that the first US gold medal of the 13th Maccabiah Games was just won by foil fencer Jeff Bukantz.

The thousand or so people at the dinner probably didn't care, but, boy, if they only knew the whole story. They were already looking forward to the next day.

But I was hoping that Fourth of July would never end. There were endless fireworks of pride and joy exploding in my head.

As of July 4, 1989, no matter what happened during the remainder of my competitive fencing career, I had duplicated one of Dad's great accomplishments. And it was in the record books forever. To a certain extent, the pressure cooker I had jumped into had subsided – at least a little bit.

I was finally able to blow off twelve years worth of steam on this wonderful Fourth of July evening.

11

Better Than Medals

Winning Dad's gold medal at the 1989 World Maccabiah Games was one of the greatest moments of my life.

But it was not even my greatest accomplishment of those Games.

In addition to being an athlete on the team, I was also the chairman of the fencing program for Maccabi USA/Sports for Israel (MUSA). Basically, that meant I was responsible for establishing the selection criteria, selecting a coach, and getting the word out in the Jewish fencing community.

Oh, and there was one other aspect of the job... fundraising. Ugh. At that time, MUSA would raise enough money to send the entire group of more than five hundred athletes to Israel. In order to accomplish this monumental task, each chair of a sport would be responsible for raising a certain amount.

If the fencing team had thirteen members, and it cost about $5,000 a head, the fencing program had a goal of around $65,000. Usually, that amount would be split between MUSA and the chair.

I raised my half by selling $100 raffles to friends, family, co-workers, and Maccabiah alumni. It was awkward, as the fundraising efforts were a hybrid of begging, cajoling, and Jewish guilt. I was very fortunate to be able to find a few ultra-generous alums who sponsored an athlete for the entire $5,000.

The team would consist of three men each in foil, epee, and saber. There were two women foilists, as well. (In 1989, neither women's epee or saber were in the Games.)

The two women were Randi Samet and sixteen-year-old Olga Chernyak.

The team was scheduled to fly to Israel at the end of June. Sometime in late May, I received a shocking and disheartening call from the MUSA office. My jaw dropped when I was told, "Jeff, one of the four countries that had entered into the women's foil event has dropped out of the Games. The rules say that no event will be held without the requisite four countries. *Please tell Randi and Olga that they aren't going to Israel and to send back their apparel packages right away.*"

I was stunned and temporarily (and uncharacteristically) speechless. I hung up the phone feeling angry and numb.

After a couple of minutes, I regained my bearings and, as was my MO, contemplated my counterattack.

Like a snorting bull about to charge, I called the President of MUSA, Bob Spivak. He answered, and much like my fencing attack, I blasted.

"Bob," I steamed, "Our motto is '**Two weeks to experience, a lifetime to remember.**' We send these kids to Israel not so much for the competition, but rather for the cultural aspects.

"Now, you're telling me that because one girl from one country pulled out, we're *not* going to send these two girls?"

Before the shell-shocked Spivak could answer, I continued ranting, "Are you willing to break these girls' hearts? For crying out loud, they have their team sweatsuits already; they're counting down the days until Israel!"

Finally, Spivak responded, "I'm sorry, but these are the rules, and we have no choice."

"Well," I said, "if you claim that we change lives by sending young adults to Israel and then demoralize these two girls because one fencer from another country pulled out, you are a *hypocrite!*"

Hearing that magic word, Spivak exploded, "I don't have to listen to this shit!" and kaboomed the receiver in my ear.

(What is it about that word, hypocrite? I once called my dad that and he didn't talk to me for two weeks! Hey, I should try that with Mom, too!)

Blatant hypocrisy aside, and after my ear stopped ringing, I had to regroup once again.

And then a lightning bolt hit me.

I remembered that Wilma Friedman, a clubmate at the FC, was studying in Sweden. Wilma had been the first alternate for the 1985 team and wanted so badly to go to Israel to visit her brother.

So, how could I ever find Wilma? Well, I also remembered that Wilma's best friend was Michelle Verhave, a Maccabiah teammate from 1981 and 1985 and fellow FC clubmate. I called Michelle, and incredibly, she had Wilma's telephone number in Sweden. YA!

I called Wilma two minutes later and, as this wild goose chase kept evolving, she answered, obviously shocked.

Now that I found Wilma, what was the grand scheme?

"Wilma," I said, "would you be able to go to Israel next month for the Games?"

"What?! Are you kidding me? Of course I'd do anything to go!," she exclaimed.

"Well, here is my plan. I want you to contact the Swedish Fencing Federation and ask if they will allow you to represent them at the Games," I went on. "If they will, tell them I will raise the necessary funds to send you."

"Okay, Jeff," she said, "I'll get back to you tomorrow."

So within a half an hour of having the President of MUSA slam the phone down in my ear, all I needed was the Swedes to give Wilma the go-ahead.

If they did, Wilma would now be the fencer representing the necessary fourth country in the women's foil event. If this miracle happened Randi Samet and Olga Chernyak would not have to return their team clothing or have their hearts broken.

I used the word "scheme" earlier. That was a mistake, as it has a negative connotation. This was a grand plan. Even for a Jew, this was the ultimate "Hail Mary." Whatever it was, it was the longest of longshots. But it was my only shot.

The next day, Wilma called and gave me the surprise answer, "Jeff, they said YES!"

I'm sure we both jumped for joy on opposite ends of that trans-Atlantic phone call.

Now I had to contact the MUSA office and let them know the great news. Needless to say, they were too shocked to be pleasantly surprised. They actually thought I was kidding.

Within twenty-four hours of the fateful news to cancel Samet and Chernyak, and the subsequent bridge-burning with Bob Spivak, I had pulled off my greatest Maccabiah victory.

There was one huge problem, though. Staying within the organization, as I hoped to do, would be impossible unless I repaired my relationship with Bob. And, as that wound had just been inflicted, it didn't look optimistic.

I decided to approach the proposed détente by injecting a little humor into the equation. Let's just say that it would take something unconventional to break the ice and start the healing.

I threw caution to the wind. My idea was to FedEx Bob a novelty and a note. The novelty was a two-inch "Hopping Pecker," and the note said, "Let's look at the big picture and not get too '*hopped*' up over the small stuff."

Well, I figured I had nothing to lose.

I received a call just after 11 a.m. the next day. It was MUSA President Bob Spivak. "Jeff, he said, "you're nuts but I loved it. Everything is fine. Thanks for your efforts."

Whew!

Bob and I became friends and occasional golf partners.

Wilma Friedman got to participate in the World Maccabiah Games and visit her brother.

Randi Samet won the bronze medal.

Young Olga Chernak won the gold medal. (In 1992, she would win the NCAA foil championship representing Penn State University.)

And I had my proudest Maccabiah moment.

12

Chutzpah, Mitzvah, and Meshugah

When I look back at my lengthy experience with Maccabi USA/Sports for Israel, it can best be summed up in two Yiddish words: **chutzpah** and **mitzvah.**

Chutzpah is nerve, brazenness.

Mitzvah is a good deed.

While winning medals and fulfilling the family legacy were always pushing my buttons, my involvement with MUSA taught me that there was something far more gratifying.

And that was giving back.

Athletes are normally self-absorbed, self-centered, and ultimately, selfish. They're focused on success, they are the kings and queens of the universe, and it is all about them. That doesn't mean they're bad people, it's just the mindset of high-level athletes while in the midst of their careers.

Luckily for me, I was asked to become involved with MUSA right after the 1985 Maccabiah Games. I was recommended by Sam Cheris, the fencing chair at the time.

I remember walking into my first conference quite nervous. I didn't know a soul, didn't know what they wanted me to do in the organization, and wasn't sure I really wanted to even get involved. However, I left that meeting knowing all the answers. It was clear to me that MUSA was in the mitzvah business. While I didn't yet learn the names of many people, the mission statement hooked me.

Maccabi USA/Sports for Israel (www.maccabiusa.com/index. htm) endeavors, through sports, to perpetuate and preserve the American Jewish community by encouraging Jewish pride, strengthening Jewish bonds and by creating a heightened awareness of Israel and Jewish identity. The volunteer organization seeks to enrich the lives of Jewish youth in the United States, Israel and the Diaspora through athletic, cultural and educational programs.

We develop, promote and support international, national and regional athletic-based activities and facilities. We strive to provide Jewish athletes the world over the opportunity to share their heritage and customs in competitive athletic settings. We support programs that embody the Maccabi ideals of Jewish continuity, Zionism and excellence in sport.

We distinguish ourselves by:

- *Sponsoring the United States Team to the World Maccabiah Games.*
- *Supporting programs such as the JCC Maccabi Games which introduce American Jewish youth to their heritage by sponsoring sports-related programs and activities.*
- *Supporting programs that enhance participation of American Jewish youth with their brethren throughout the world.*
- *Supporting athletic facilities and programs in Israel.*
- *Being a member of Maccabi World Union and worldwide Maccabi movement.*

Let me be clear about this: I am not religious. I am proud to be a Jew, and embrace the cultural and traditional aspects of the religion. As the son of a Holocaust survivor, I don't have to be religious to know that Jews will always be the 'chosen ones,' at least from those in the world who choose to persecute.

So MUSA's mission, which was basically to expose Jewish youth to both Israel and their identity, hit home with me.

I decided to take an active role in the organization. In 1986, I was named chair of fencing for 13th Games, which would take place in July 1989.

At the same time, of course, I was knee-deep in my competitive career and trying to make the team. I was concerned that the distraction of fundraising and planning would hamper my results, but it didn't, as I earned the #2 ranking (my highest ever) that season.

As per the last chapter, my first mitzvah was pulling off the Wilma Friedman miracle. That's as good as it gets, and I've never felt more *nachas*. (Yiddish for "pride, joy, gratification.")

It took a lot of chutzpah to get Wilma to represent Sweden, which enabled our two girls to go to Israel. But I saved a little chutzpah for myself.

This would be my third and final Maccabiah Games, and it would be nice to go out with a little notoriety. (There, Eric, I admit it!) So, I decided to call the head of the entire team, Jeffrey Laikind, and make my case.

"Jeff," I reasoned, "when it comes to selecting the athletes who carry the flag or the banners to lead the team into the opening ceremonies, you always choose a popular sport. Fencing never gets any recognition."

I continued, "As a second generation gold-medalist (the 1985 epee gold, remember?), I think I deserve some consideration."

Jeffrey Laikind, probably stunned by this show of chutzpah, replied, "I'll take it under consideration. Please fax me your competitive resumé."

Lo and behold, that heaping dose of chutzpah paid off. Jeffrey Laikind performed a mitzvah and named me as one of the five athletes who would have the honor or leading the team into Ramat Gan Stadium on July 3, 1989.

I'll never forget marching in, proudly holding the blue and white **Maccabi USA** banner along with Olympic rower Sherri Cassuto, and having a painted-on smile that probably made me look like Jack Nicholson's portrayal of "The Joker."

I felt like I was walking on air. Maybe I was, as I won the gold medal twenty-four hours later.

Best of all, however, was that I had raised the funds for the fencing team and enabled twelve athletes and two coaches to go to Israel for **'Two weeks to experience, a lifetime to remember.'**

I was named as chair of fencing for the 14th Games, to be held in July, 1993. By this time, my career was winding down, and I actually looked forward to the fundraising. Only this time, I decided to turn the unpleasant task into a fun one.

In order to accomplish that, it was chutzpah time.

Anyone can sell $100 raffles. Some can score $5,000 sponsor-an-athlete donations. But for the "Melech (Hebrew for king) of Chutzpah", it would take something different... something special... something unique.

And, **Maccabiah Mania I**, *'Grappling for Gelt'* was born. Yes, in order to raise the funds for the 1993 team, I would promote a professional wrestling show. The show would feature some legends such as Killer Kowalski, Baron von Raschke, The Iron Sheik, Iron Mike Sharpe, and my good buddy Ken Patera.

There were even two female wrestlers, Misty Blue and Linda Dallas, who would use my daughter Stephanie's room as a dressing room.

As a lifelong fan of this nonsense, I would also get to live out a fantasy by participating in a match. I needed a character, as plain old Jeff Bukantz wouldn't cut it. Neither would The

Melech of Chutzpah. Nor would The John McEnroe of
Fencing. (Although that had some potential.)

Instead, I became the masked **Mighty Maccabee**, also
known as the **Hebrew Hammer**. Unlike my spandex singlet,
the name fit perfectly.

In preparation for my rasslin' debut, I went down to Brick
Township to train at Iron Mike Sharpe's school. Yes, I left the
world of chutzpah and entered The Twilight Zone!

On the day before the show, I received a call from Baron
Mikel Scicluna. Without any fanfare or build-up, Scicluna
growled, "I'm not coming tomorrow."

"Why not, Baron?" I asked.

"Because my friend Davey O'Hannon told me not to,
that's why!" The Baron barked.

Davey O'Hannon? Dangerous Davey O'Hannon? Why
was this former jobber (another word for designated loser)
involved here?

So I immediately called my friend Jonathan Gold, who was
responsible for procuring the talent. "Jon, I just got this weird
call from Scicluna, who said he's not coming. When I asked
him why, he said Davey O'Hannon told him not to."

Gold knew right away this was bad and lamented, "Oh,
this is not good. O'Hannon and I have heat with each other
from the past, and he must have gotten word that I was
involved in this show."

Gold gave me O'Hannon's number and I called him. "Hello,
this is Jeff Bukantz. I'm holding the show in Livingston tomorrow
and I got a call from Scicluna saying you had a problem."

O'Hannon didn't mince words, "Listen, I don't know
you but here's the deal: I don't like Jon Gold. You don't have
a license for tomorrow's show. I'm calling the state to have it
closed down."

Before either one could hang up on the other, I responded,
"Look, here's the deal. I am having a private party by invitation
only. It is not open to the public. The state has no jurisdiction

over anything. I've done nothing to you and you have no right to do anything to me."

O'Hannon, tougher on the phone than he was in the ring, just said, "Oh, we'll see about that!" and slammed down the receiver.

I called Gold to fill him in and then called Ken Patera. Patera, in addition to being a 1972 Olympic weightlifter, went on to become one of the biggest stars in wrestling. We met in January 1978 at a show in Miami at the Orange Bowl and became lifelong friends.

Patera laughed when I told him about O'Hannon's threat and said, "Give me his number, I'll work it out."

Five minutes later, he did. Scicluna, out of loyalty to O'Hannon, was a no-show. O'Hannon, out of respect for Patera, thankfully was a no-show, as well.

The event would be held under a giant tent in the cul-de-sac in front of my house.

I was able to have the town of Livingston close off the street for the event. I had hired professional sound people, a television crew, and two announcers.

Sunday, April 4, 1993 finally arrived. About three hundred of my friends and family were there, shivering on that chilly day at the outdoor Bukantz Square Garden.

The fur was flying that day. It was hectic. I was responsible for everything, from greeting people, to paying people, to actually wrestling. I was a bit frazzled.

And then, out of the blue, a red-faced Fire Chief Craig Dufford came up to me and matter-of-factly announced, "We're closing you down."

"WHAT?!" I asked and exclaimed at the same time.

The Chief said, "There is a car parked illegally on the street, and it's a fire hazard."

At that point, I wanted to say, "You stupid jerk, whose salary is paid by my taxes, why don't you just have the person move the car instead of threatening to close me down?"

But somehow I realized that would not have brought the desired result. So, in my best schoolboy voice, I sheepishly asked, "Chief, if I get the car moved and make an announcement that that part of the street is off-limits for parking, would that be okay?"

"Well," Chief Dufford assured, "If that car isn't moved in five minutes, the show is closed down."

And with that, he turned and walked away.

The car was moved, and the fire started by the Chief was put out. It was a bit of a false alarm, wouldn't you say?

So, after the threats to shut me down by both Dangerous Davey O'Hannon and Livingston Fire Chief Dufford were averted, the show went on.

Friends and family from all parts of my life were there.

Even Maccabi USA's Bob Spivak and Ron Carner were there. Pretty impressive, considering they had flown overnight from Israel and arrived at JFK airport earlier that morning!

In the main event, Ken Patera and The Mighty Maccabee defeated The Iron Sheik and Iron Mike Sharpe when The Maccabee pinned Sharpe. (What, you thought I was going to lose?)

But the big winner that day was MUSA, as I raised about $20,000. A little chutzpah led to a lot of mitzvah. Actually, the plural is mitzvot. That summer, thirteen athletes and one coach traveled to Israel for "**Two weeks to experience, a lifetime to remember.**"

* * *

Naturally, this left MUSA with no choice but to name me as chair for the 15th Games, to be held in 1997.

I decided to risk my undefeated record and promote **Maccabiah Mania II, '*Shekel Slam*'.**

As Bukantz Square Garden was unavailable (well, that's what my wife Carol told me), this event would be held at the Livingston High School main gym on Saturday, March 1, 1997.

Or, so I thought.

While on the way to Newark Airport on Friday afternoon to pick up my camp buddy Tom Rosenberg, Kamala (The Ugandan Giant), and The Iron Sheik, I received a phone call from someone at the high school.

He said I did not have the proper insurance paperwork from MUSA and that they were canceling my show. Just... like... that.

This was like the banquet hall calling the night before the wedding or Bar Mitzvah and telling you the event was off. While Maccabiah Mania II was not as important as a wedding or a Bar Mitzvah, the effort and expense was the same. There were three hundred and fifty to four hundred people coming the next day!

Fortunately, Rosenberg's plane arrived first. Tom and I became great friends while at Camp Scatico in the late 70's. In 1976, we were opposing generals in the grand finale of the summer: Color War. Thirty years later, it still gives me great pleasure to remind him whose team won. Tom is a top-notch attorney, even if he can't win an argument with me. (He actually handled John Kerry's 2004 election issues in Ohio.)

Although it was now about 5:30 p.m. on a Friday, we were able to contact the person at the high school. Very lucky!

Tom did his magic on the cell phone, and what was cancelled at 4:30 p.m. was back on by 6 p.m.

That's what friends are for.

We then went to pick up Kamala, the four hundred-pound giant who was not from Uganda, but rather truck-driving James Harris from Mississippi. On this day, however, his name was Mud, as the skunk no-showed the flight, never called, and didn't return the ticket.

What a jerk.

No big deal; he was in a minor match anyway.

On to the next and most important pick-up, The Iron Sheik, the former WWF Champion. He would be The Mighty

Maccabee's opponent in the main event, the match everyone was waiting for.

Tom and I held our breath and waited for The Sheik. Everyone came off the plane, but no Sheik. This afternoon had become a nightmare. Finally, a bandana-wearing and limping Iron Sheik was the final passenger to come out of the gate.

The last hurdle had been cleared. Or so I thought.

As we walked from the gate to baggage claim, The Iron Sheik held me up for an extra $500 to do the match with me the next day. After the near-cancellation of my show and the Kamala no-show, $500 was a small price to pay by this time.

And, so I did.

There was only one other problem on game day, as Bam Bam Bigelow didn't want to sign the photos I was giving out to those who shelled out $100 for the event. Well, what would you expect from a guy with tattoos of fire on the top of his head? Another jerk.

Other than that, everything went like clockwork.

My daughter Stephanie sounded like an angel when she sang *The Star-Spangled Banner*.

My son Michael introduced The Mighty Maccabee into the ring.

Bruce Jugan flew in from California, David Weissman and Terrence Gargiulo drove down from Boston, and Russell Wilson drove up from Washington, DC. Lots of Camp Scatico friends were there, as well.

And, as in 1993, Bob Spivak and Ron Carner showed their support. MUSA's Joy Gordon, who had helped me with publicity, was there, too.

Classy Freddie Blassie sang his 1970's cult hit, "Pencil Neck Geek." (Appropriately, Eric Rosenberg played the role of the pencil neck geek.)

Nikolai Volkoff sang "Cara Mia" and "Hava Nagila."

Superfly Jimmy Snuka flew off of the top rope onto his hapless opponent.

King Kong Bundy, reached at 4 a.m., replaced the Ugandan lowlife, Kamala.

And, yes, The Mighty Maccabee pinned The Iron Sheik to win the World Maccabiah Championship. The match included brutal chair shots and lots of outside interference, but ended when The Maccabee jumped off of the second rope and clobbered The Sheik on the top of his bald head with my steel-meshed fencing mask.

As The Maccabee was not used to 'pulling the shot,' the mask to the head left a nasty-looking bloody waffle on The Sheik's skull. In the locker-room, he was not pleased, to put it mildly. Let's just say it was a 'receipt' for the extra $500 he scammed from me.

(Actually, The Iron Sheik was very professional. He used to wrestle Hulk Hogan in front of 22,000 fans at Madison Square Garden. Now, in the twilight of his career, he was gracious enough to work his butt off at Livingston High School before a few hundred. He gave his trademark cartoon-character interviews, didn't hurt me in the ring, and allowed me to pin him. He deserved the extra $500.)

Maccabiah Mania II, Shekel Slam, was a huge hit. It helped raise about $30,000 for MUSA and the 1997 Maccabiah fencing team.

It was a mitzvah for fourteen athletes and one coach, as they went to Israel for **"Two weeks to experience, a lifetime to remember."**

While The Mighty Maccabee retired in 1997 from active competition, he is still available for personal appearances at autograph signings, birthday parties, and Bar Mitzvot.

However, now that I've been reappointed to chair the fencing program for the 18th Games in July, 2009, it will be back to the fundraising grind.

Is there any chutzpah left? Will there be a Maccabiah Mania III?

Could this mean the long-awaited return of the undefeated Mighty Maccabee?

All I know is that The Mighty Maccabee lives for the mitzvah.

Time for a new and larger spandex singlet, that's for sure!

Oh, you might be wondering about the third word in the chapter title, *'meshugah.'*

Well, that is the Yiddish word for: crazy.

And that makes me a *'meshuggener.'*

13

Like Making the New York Yankees

In addition to all of his individual accomplishments, Dad was also known as a tremendous team fencer. In four Olympic Games, he had an outstanding seventy percent win-loss ratio in the team events. He even had a 5-2 win over Eduardo Mangiarotti in the semifinal match against Italy in 1956; Mangiarotti has the most fencing medals in Olympic history. As I mentioned before, in 1958 he beat the four Soviets who went on to win the next two Olympic Team gold medals.

When my dad was a top fencer, it was considered a great honor in the United States to win the National Team Championship. Naturally, Dad was the anchor of the New York Fencers Club (NYFC) Team. During his era, he led the NYFC to the National Championships a record nine times.

Even when it came to the footsteps he left in team competitions, my dad's legacy again seemed impossible for me to fill.

But first things first: Before I could compete on the team, I had to make the team, the NYFC Team, just like my dad. This was no easy task, as the NYFC was loaded with the best foil fencers in the country, let alone the city. As it was referred to in the fencing community, making the NYFC foil team was "like making the New York Yankees."

By 1979 I had broken out of my shell, but the NYFC Team was loaded with veterans who were ranked above me. I would have to be patient.

I continued to improve in 1980, and my results in the Opens vaulted me to the #1 spot in the Metropolitan Division's foil point standings. I was a hot rock, training four nights a week. I knew it was my time. When it came to select the 1980 NYFC Team, I never thought for a second that I'd be passed over, but I was.

Why was there a hurdle every step of the way? Why was nothing in my fencing career easy to come by? I was becoming paranoid that I was being held to a higher standard than the other fencers – or maybe resented – simply because I was Danny Bukantz's son.

The captain of the NYFC foil team in 1980 was Olympian John Nonna, whose decision it was to offer Neal Cohen the fourth and final spot on the team. Cohen was an excellent fencer who had almost won the individual title in 1974. However, he hadn't trained all season long until the few last weeks before the nationals.

In comparison, I had practiced three to four times a week – every week! – since the Fencers Club opened the day after Labor Day. I had proven myself a winner by becoming the stud of the season in the Metropolitan Division.

Cohen, however, brought something to the team, I guess, that was deemed more important: he had been a member of the NYFC Team for many years, including the defending 1979 National Championship team. When push came to shove, Nonna went for experience.

It was hard to argue with his decision, although an argument can be made that the best young rookie deserved

Dr. Daniel Bukantz, *Olympian Extraordinaire*

1952 US Olympic Team to Helsinki

Dad with 1948 Olympic foil champion Jehan Buhan
and referee F. Barnard O'Connor at the black-tie
exhibition at the New York Fencers Club in 1951

After his signature counter-four parry, Dad riposting
right in the middle of Buhan's chest

Dad embracing 1952 & 1956 Olympic foil champion
Christian D'Oriola at another exhibition at
the Fencers Club

Hey, Dad, Mom says you should have pulled up
your socks!

Win or lose, make sure you shake the referee's hand!
Guess who lost?

Mom with, as Nat Lubell called me, "The Chinaman"

The three-year-old prodigy… who needs knickers
anyway?

Mom, Dad, and me on my Bar Mitzvah day in
September, 1970

Dad zipping me up at my first New York Open in 1974 at the NYAC… he was right, I wasn't ready!

After the 1980 snub from the NYFC team, scoring the national championship touch against Salle Auriol's Pat Gerard in 1981 in Fort Worth, Texas… and filling one of Dad's footsteps

Also in 1981, in my first US National final, hitting
8-time champion Mike Marx in the flank with my
infamous "lunge"

At the 1987 Pan American Games in Indianapolis,
my beloved coaches Simon Pinkhasov and the late
Csaba Elthes

JUNE, 1958

American Fencing

NATIONAL
CHAMPIONSHIPS

Hotel Commodore, N.Y.
June 29 through July 5

DEFENDING CHAMPIONS

JANICE LEE ROMARY
Women's Foil

RICHARD BERRY
Epee

DR. DANIEL BUKANTZ
Foil

DANIEL MAGAY
Sabre

—Photo by Asuc

Vol. 9   No.

Official Publication of the Amateur Fencers League of America

Cover of *American Fencing* magazine; June 1958.
Dad defends national foil title

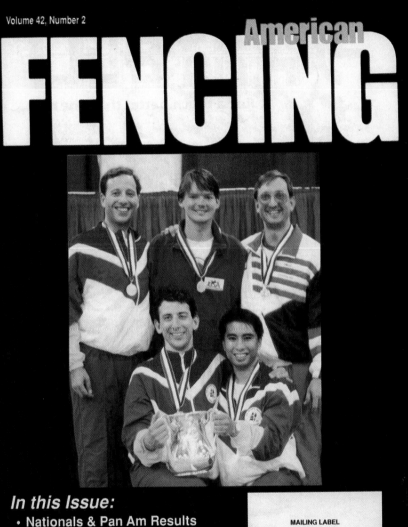

Volume 42, Number 2

American
FENCING

In this Issue:
- Nationals & Pan Am Results
- The Fencer's Survival Kit
- Direct for Success

MAILING LABEL

Cover of *American Fencing* magazine; 1991.
Jeff with NYFC teammates Jerome Demarque,
Jack Tichaek, Nat Cohen, and Al Carlay after winning
the national foil team trophy

On July 3, 1989, carrying the Maccabi USA banner into the Opening Ceremonies of the 13th World Maccabiah Games at Ramat Gan Stadium in Israel

On July 4, 1989, finally atop the Maccabiah podium having won the foil gold medal Dad won in 1950… another footstep filled!

I never wore my medals… definitely not cool… except this one time

Hurry up, fellas, there are no FIE muckety-mucks
watching!

Finally getting the call to ref the Olympic foil finals
in Atlanta, 1996. Forget filling another footstep,
where's my change of underwear?

In 1997, The Mighty Maccabee won the belt
and more importantly, raised the gelt

"Iron"ically, the Iranian bad guy, The Iron Sheik,
helped me raise about $45,000 for the 1993 and 1997
US Maccabiah fencing teams

Marching in to the 2004 Opening Ceremonies in
Athens… another footstep filled… these people all
came to see me?

At the Athens press conference after predicting – I
mean, guaranteeing – the US would win a gold
and a bronze medal, at least!

Mom and Jeff at Mom's 80th birthday party, May 15, 2004... one day before Mike Moran suggested that American athletes do not celebrate with the flag in Athens (Darling, you looked magnificent!)

How many people can say they've rubbed elbows with George Bush #41 and The Iron Sheik #1?

At adidas House in Athens, modeling with the
mannequins

On August 17, 2004, the US Olympic Team throwing
Olympic Champion Mariel Zagunis into the rarified air;
Mariel holding Mom's flag... take that, Mike Moran!

Alice Bukantz

Three generations of Camp Scatico Bukantzes;
Stephanie (1994-2005), Jeff (1974-79), Uncle Bob in
back, Dad (1938-40), Michael (1996-present),
and Carol (1978-79)

August 2, 2004; Dad introducing me
and presenting me the plaque at the Hall of
Fame ceremony… what a footstep filled!

Mom, Dad, and Jeff

the shot and needed to get the experience, as well. The NYFC
Team ended up winning another championship in 1980, with
Cohen being a key contributor to the team.

But I was still crushed. I had worked my ass off all year
to improve and had earned a spot on that team. Despite the
demoralizing snub by Nonna, I did what I always did; I went
to practice at the club on the day after Labor Day (1980), the
traditional opening night of the new season. By chance, one of
the first people I ran into that night was Nonna.

I had an entire summer's worth of anger built up inside,
and I told Nonna that I resented his decision to include Cohen
on the team over me. I told him that I believed I deserved
the spot on the team based on becoming one of the strongest
fencers in the area, let alone in the club. I continued my
cathartic rant by telling him that the snub was completely
unfair considering I had trained since the first day of the season
and Cohen trained for barely a month leading up to Nationals.
Nonna wasn't in the mood for this confrontation and basically
blew me off. After he let Cohen know about my comments,
neither one of them spoke to me for the rest of the season,
which, at that point, was fine by me. By ignoring me, they were
only giving me the added incentive to push myself harder. I was
determined to make the team in 1981. I was also determined
to kick their asses in the individual competitions as well.

As it turned out, 1981 was my breakout year on the
National Circuit; I ended the season as the sixth-ranked foil
fencer in the country. There was no possible way that I could
be denied my rightful spot on the NYFC Team that year.

This time, I finally got the nod.

Now, as the two-time defending championship team,
there was an atypical pressure on the members of the NYFC
foil team: anything less than first place was considered a total
failure. Talk about being thrown into the fire!

I started on the team and won most of my bouts ending
up 11-2 for the competition. Believe me, I was winning these

bouts with the team's best interests in mind, but I was also doing everything possible to show Nonna he had made a mistake the previous year.

For the gold medal match, we drew the Salle Auriol team from Portland, Oregon. This team boasted the best fencer in the country: Mike Marx. In addition, they had two wily veterans in Pat Gerard and Pierre Des Georges, and Marx's brother Robert, a world-class epee fencer.

In my first team event, I shocked everyone by beating Mike Marx. And, for the record, the winning touch was straight out of a dream. I caught Marx in Ol' Faithful, the counter-four parry; however, I then threw in a wrinkle by riposting not to Marx's chest, where he would undoubtedly be waiting with his own parry, but rather to his flank (under his right arm). I surprised everyone in the room, including myself, with that once-in-a-lifetime touch. In the deciding bout, I beat Gerard to win the National Team Championship for the NYFC. I was mobbed by my teammates – including Nonna – and all was forgotten about the previous year's snub as we took in the moment.

I had finally "made the New York Yankees."

I had finally become a national champion, albeit in a team event.

And, best of all, I duplicated one of Dad's accomplishments.

But he won the team championship nine times; this was only my first. Even if I never won it again, though, I had followed in Danny Bukantz's footsteps. Maybe I had only filled a toe, but it was in the record books forever.

At the moment we won the gold medal I celebrated with my new teammates, but after the moment was over, I still felt like an outsider. Nonna, McCahey, and Tichacek were a clique because they had all been stars before I hit the scene. Whether the snub was perceived or real, I definitely felt alienated from my Fencers Club teammates.

While they hung out pretty exclusively with one another at the competition, I had become pretty good friends with Jim Bonacorda, Ed McNamara, and Jim Powers. All three were members of the NYFC's archrival: the New York Athletic Club, or as some call it, the "New York Anti-Semitic Club."

In fact, I sometimes traveled with them to NACs. I was just much closer to these guys than I was with the members of my own team. Actually, come to think of it, I wasn't close at all with my teammates – except for Eric Rosenberg. We had something in common, as we both felt like outsiders within our own club.

McNamara was my best buddy from the NYAC. We really bonded. So it wasn't a surprise me when he approached me and asked if I'd like the join the NYAC and represent his club.

You see, in 1981, the team events were increased from three fencers to four. The NYFC, naturally, was four fencers deep already, but the NYAC only had three: my buddies Powers, McNamara, and Bonacorda. Thus, the NYFC – my team – was already a great team, and the NYAC – their team – was a very good team. But they wanted very badly to become a great team; they wanted very badly to overtake the NYFC for both intra-city and national bragging rights.

In 1981 and 1982, they made a full court press to get me to switch teams. They felt that the balance of power would tilt if I made the decision to leave the NYFC for the NYAC. I was really tempted and naturally very flattered. And, contrary to the alienation I often felt from my NYFC teammates, I felt wanted by the guys at the NYAC.

By this time, the NYAC had changed substantially since the day my dad was asked to join – but only if he claimed on the membership form that he wasn't Jewish. In the early '80s the NYAC had some token Jews as members. There were still no women or black members, but there were a few Jews.

But there was still a problem. You see, I had competed at the NYAC many times. I had refereed there as well. I had even practiced with my friends there every Wednesday night for an entire season. Yet every time I walked into that building, something didn't feel right about it. My mom was a Holocaust survivor, and my dad had been asked to deny his faith by the club. To be frank, whenever I was there, my skin crawled. Without denigrating any member of the NYAC, the fact remained that at one point it was inherently anti-Semitic.

So, as a proud Jew, I decided I just couldn't join the NYAC. It was a matter of principle. I could live with being an outsider in the NYFC clique. But I could never live with being an outsider within a club based on my religion.

Without striving to do so, I followed in my dad's footsteps in this case; I stayed with the NYFC.

As a testament to the trio from the NYAC, they remained good friends with me even after I turned down their offer. I will always have a warm spot in my heart for McNamara, Powers, and Bonacorda. Best of all, as the years went by and the competition died down, I did become close with McCahey and Tichacek. I consider them two of the best friends I made in the sport.

From 1981 until 1994, I was the only fencer to represent the NYFC at the National Team Championships every year. I had many outstanding teammates – Nonna, Jack Tichacek, Michael McCahey, Peter Lewison, Eric Rosenberg, Jerome Demarque, Nat Cohen, Al Carlay, Lew Siegel, Philippe Bennett, Phil Mathis, Rob Conway, Dan Kellner, and John Troiano. But over a span of fourteen years, I was the only constant. I also experienced a career's worth of ups and downs competing for the NYFC foil team.

I'd won a National Championship deciding bout, but I'd lost one as well. Each championship brought new and unexpected challenges. And, we would consider anything less than the gold medal as an outright failure. In that respect, the NYFC Team was just like the New York Yankees; it was win or bust.

While we all wanted to make an Olympic Team, Pan Am Team, World University Team, or World Championship Team, we always looked at the National Championship Team as the focal point of the entire season. My teammates and I were proud to represent the NYFC, and we would accept nothing less than a first-place finish.

Of course, I was the only second generation member of the NYFC Team, which meant that I was the only member of the team whose Dad had won nine team championships of his own. And that meant that I felt an additional dose of pressure that none of my teammates could ever comprehend. That pressure led me to help win eight National Championships. During the fourteen years I competed as a member of the NYFC Team, I won more than half of my bouts in gold medal matches.

I still believe that I should have been on the 1980 NYFC Team, which would have given me a ninth title in fifteen years. But, okay, eight was more than enough. At the end of the day, I was kind of glad that my dad had one more team championship than I did. He stands on a pedestal that I'm thrilled and honored to look up at.

In 2004, after my parents had already left for their winter home in Sarasota, I went over to their Forest Hills apartment and opened the medal case that Dad's late friend Frank Bavuso had hand-made for him. I took out the nine US National Team Championship medals.

When I got back to my house I put together a brand new display case. In this new case, the seventeen National Team Championship medals won by my dad and me while representing the NYFC were displayed together. Our combined seventeen gold medals is a record that will never be broken. They are family footsteps that will never be filled by anyone else. And nothing makes me happier than to know that medal case hangs in my dad's study, which used to be my room. I can't imagine how proud he is of his son. Danny Bukantz's son.

14

Dueling Can Be Grueling

Playing any sport can lead to injuries. Competing at the national and international levels, when everything becomes much more than just a "game," exponentially increases the odds of becoming bruised and beaten.

Fencing is a combat sport. It's a one-on-one sport. The blades are made of maraging (generally unbreakable) steel. Tests have shown that fencing blades can be wielded at speeds of over one hundred miles per hour.

When you're hit with a stiff thrust, you feel it. Even through the Kevlar uniform, you feel it. Remember the poor Israeli epee fencer I sent to the hospital at the 1985 Maccabiah Games?

In addition, sometimes you're hit with a whipping action that often hurts much more than the common thrusts. Most male fencers don't wear protective cups because they are uncomfortable and restrictive. I can attest that a swift whip to the groin area results in a slightly delayed reaction. When that pain comes, you feel like passing out right there on the strip.

The worst part of fencing is getting into the shower after a competition or rough practice. When the water hits the fresh abrasions, scrapes, and bruises, it stings like hell.

While fencing, your feet are always moving and changing direction. They take a beating; you're guaranteed to develop all sorts of raw blisters before they eventually "heal" and become thick calluses.

Your fingers aren't necessarily safe, either. As you grip the weapon and make the routine movements, you also get nasty blisters on certain fingers. Some of your knuckles will become mangled, particularly your index finger, which rubs against the inside of the protective bell (the protective cover around your hand). I know identical twin sisters from Rochester, New York, named Hanna and Metta Thompson. I simply can't tell them apart, which is a little embarrassing whenever I referee or captain for them. So, I use the ol' noodle to tell them apart. You see, Hanna is a lefty and Metta is a righty. When I greet either one, I don't try to make eye contact, but instead look directly at their hands. Based on which hand has the gnarly knuckle, I've got my Thompson!

Fencers make plosive actions with their legs all the time; twisted ankles, hamstring pulls, and groin injuries are common.

Fencers make plosive actions with their fencing arms all the time; tennis elbow is prevalent and wrist injuries commonplace.

My career has been rife with injuries that run the gamut from minor to very major.

My first real injury happened in 1976 as I was fencing Tom Veljacic in the Under-19 National Championship qualifier at the Fencers Club. On one action, we both attacked. Our bells crashed with an impressive clang.

Right away, I knew something was wrong. My left index finger had been completely broken. The pain was bad, but worse was losing the grip strength to hold my foil. So I taped my hand and foil together and finished the tournament. Yep!

Just like a hockey player would do.

A few years later, in either 1979 or 1980, I faced a pretty serious injury. I was practicing at the New York Athletic Club, as I often did that season on Wednesday nights. While fencing old friend McNamara, I attacked him with a fleche. In the middle of the move, as my back right leg crossed in front of my left, I felt a pop – right in my groin area. The pain was worse than anything I had ever before felt. I was immobile. It ended up being a grade-3 tear, the most serious kind of tear, of my right pectineus muscle – one of the adductor muscles in the groin.

It took what seemed like a month to limp to the train station that night. And it really did take a month of rehab before I could get back on the fencing strip.

Fencers are always lunging and fleching, so there are many obvious risks of suffering groin injuries. For the rest of my career, the pectineus muscle would be like a "Sword of Damocles" hanging over my head. Before every practice or competition, I would go through very lengthy and very tedious stretching exercises.

I'd never been very limber; this injury only made it worse. My clubmates amused themselves during that time by watching me warm up. Even at national competitions, other fencers would gather around my warm-up area to see me – the freak of nature – attempt to stretch.

I sustained two additional injuries that were direct results of my own temper and stupidity.

At the 1982 Michel Alaux NAC in New York City, I was really pissed off after losing a tough bout. (Then again, I was always pissed whenever I lost.) In a sheer display of a terribly bad temper, I took my foil into my right hand, held it by the blade, and forcefully slam-dunked it onto the floor.

Ordinarily, this would have made me feel much better. I figured that I was punishing the foil for causing me to lose the bout. Only this time, the weapon punished me!

As it turned out, there was a tiny burr of steel protruding from the side of the blade. When I fired the blade onto the ground, that tiny little burr ripped apart my thumb.

There was blood everywhere. My thumb was busted wide open.

I felt like an idiot. Well, I was an idiot.

Before my next bout started I had to get stitched up by Dr. Karen Brynildsen. The thought of it made me nauseated. I turned pale, broke into a cold sweat, and nearly threw up.

But, just like a hockey player, I went right back into the battle.

I learned a very important lesson from that incident. In the future, I would always remember to only throw my foils with my *gloved* hand.

The other self-inflicted injury really epitomized both my temper and stupidity.

In 1983 I was fencing in a New Jersey Open at Montclair Kimberly Academy. In the pecking order of important events, this one was definitely at the bottom. Nevertheless, once I entered a competition, it didn't matter to me how important the event was or wasn't. I always arrived on the strip in ill humor; I viewed each bout as a life-or-death situation.

In the semi-final pool of six, I lost a bout to Fencers Club teammate Dr. Gary Pepper. Pepper was a tough cookie and well-seasoned, but I shouldn't have lost to him. That's the way I saw it, anyway.

After the bout, I stormed out of the gym into the adjacent hallway. Without thinking, I punched the wall as hard as I could. Have you ever noticed the walls of school hallways? Pure cinderblock.

I think my brain was made of pure cinderblock that day too. Not only did I punch a cinderblock wall as hard as possible, I did it with my left hand – my fencing hand!

Idiot!

I'm not sure if the hand was actually broken, but some of those little bones must have been shattered. I was too embarrassed to go see a doctor. I just took a week off and somehow got away with yet another temper-provoked lack of judgment.

And, yes, I learned from this painful mistake as well. In the future I knew to only punch walls with my *right* hand.

To add insult to injury, my buddy Jim Powers of the NYAC came up to me in the gym shortly after the wall-punching incident and accused me of throwing the bout to my teammate, Pepper. Luckily for Powers, my left hand – my punching hand – was temporarily out of order.

To this day, Powers insists I gave Pepper the bout. "There was no way you should have lost to him," Powers always said with a smirk.

Well, yeah! That's why I punched the damn wall in the first place.

Along the way there were bouts – no pun intended – of wrist and shoulder tendonitis. These injuries were nagging, as opposed to debilitating, but they all took their toll on my body and my psyche.

However, there was one type of tendonitis that was extremely serious, and it was in my elbow. Yes – the dreaded tennis elbow.

The combination of gripping the weapon with my fingers and the rapid extension of my arm during an action, where the arm straightens out, led to a tennis elbow that just wouldn't heal. I went to the most famous sports doctors in New York, including Russell Warren of the New York Giants. After years of rehab, rest, and Cortisone shots, the damn elbow just wouldn't get better.

For those of you who've never had a serious case of tennis elbow, consider yourself blessed. Without getting too graphic, let's just say that the pain is unbearable. It hurts. All. The. Time.

You can't pick up a book, no matter how light, using your fingers.

You can't push the top of the shaving cream can without getting a shooting pain right to the elbow.

For crying out loud! It's nearly impossible to wipe yourself.

The severe case of tennis elbow often left me in tears of frustration and pain. I seriously contemplated quitting the sport. There were times I entertained the idea of trying to fence right-handed. That's how desperate I was!

Sometimes the tennis elbow would seem to get a little better. Then I'd make one explosive move and the elbow would blow up again. It was wearing me down.

The worst it ever felt was after a tournament in Atlanta. I won the tournament and was celebrating with a bottle of champagne at dinner with Atlanta Fencers Club coach Gene Gettler. I drank the entire bottle, stuck my elbow in the ice bucket, and, despite trying to numb myself with alcohol and ice, my elbow continued to throb.

Tennis elbow was an injury that would stay with me for the last six or seven years of my competitive career. I was at the rehab clinic so often that they probably named a wing of the facility in my honor.

I used to think that losing weight would be my biggest problem in fencing, but that was something I could – and learned to – control. The ever-present injuries, however, were something I couldn't control. For a casual athlete, this would have been extremely frustrating, but for a world-class athlete, these injuries had the potential to derail a career or at least severely hamper performance. (Take it easy fellas, "world-class" was used just for emphasis, not for self-aggrandizement!)

I just learned to deal with the pain, which never really lessened in severity.

For me, the injuries were a perpetual pain in the ass. Just one more hurdle to overcome.

15

Jeffrey, Darling...

Earlier I called my mom, Alice, a Holocaust survivor. I used that term as a means of being descriptive, and not in any way to suggest that she was defined solely by those words. Unfortunately, after I wrote an article in which I said I was the son of a dentist father and a Holocaust survivor mother, Mom became upset by the (mis)characterization and told me why:

"Is that all I am? A Holocaust survivor?" she asked.

Before I could answer, I was given my answer. "I have accomplished many things in my life, and surviving the Holocaust is not among them. That's not who I am!"

Of course she was right. While I hope Mom understood that I didn't intend to suggest that's all she's ever been, it may have come out that way. And for that, Mom, I'm truly sorry.

Alice Ellenbogen was born on May 15, 1924 (okay, Mom, the Jack Benny 39+ age game is over) to Malvina and Julius in Nove Zamky, Czechoslovakia. Nove Zamky, or "New Castles," a city that dates backs to 1545, was basically obliterated by three massive air bombings during World War II in 1944 and 1945.

Mom was the oldest of three children. Robert was the middle child and Clara was the youngest. They were a beautiful family that was forever separated when the Nazis marched into Nove Zamky and removed the Ellenbogens from their home, packed them like sardines into a rancid cattle car, and deposited them in a concentration camp. The five walked to the entrance of the camp together – for the very last time – and were separated at the gate. Mom's parents were forced in one direction, she and her siblings in another.

Mercifully, the three children, ranging from sixteen to twenty years old at the time, survived. After being liberated by the Allied Forces, the shell-shocked trio was able to board a ship to America in the hopes of starting a new life.

Mom learned English and graduated from the Fashion Institute of Technology in New York City. She went on to become the top designer for dressmaker Anne Klein.

In the mid-1950s, my father's dental school classmate Mark Grossman introduced the pair, and on April 29, 1956, Alice Ellenbogen became Alice Bukantz. (And, as my dad would kid years later when he and Mom had a tiff, "My EX-friend Mark Grossman!")

Little Jeffrey was born on September 17, 1957. On that day Anne Klein's top designer traded in her job for a much more important one, that of mother.

While this memoir is about the pursuit of my dad's legacy, it shouldn't imply that I love and respect my mom any less than I do my dad. The reality is that Mom was mainly responsible for raising me, teaching me, and coddling me through my formative years. When I look back at the unyielding drive and will to win that I possessed, I fully credit those positive traits to my mom.

Whenever I've asked her about the Holocaust and how she views its effect on her life, she's always responded, "There is no question that the Nazis ruined the lives of our family. But, I decided that I would never let them ruin the rest of my life. If I allowed that to happen, it would have allowed them to ultimately defeat me."

"I decided," she continued, "to live my life to the fullest. That would be my revenge."

Whew! It's not easy to type those words, no matter how strong Mom has been or how incredible an attitude she has always displayed throughout her extraordinary life.

I don't mean to trivialize her experience by suggesting my will to succeed and overcome obstacle, in any way, compares to hers. I'm just trying to illustrate how my personal makeup is largely similar to my mom's.

As I grew up and started going to school, Mom became Dad's dental assistant. Her ebullient personality lit up the office, and I'm sure his patients appreciated her warmth. (Even if it did test my dad's "patience" at times...)

When I look back on my fencing career, Mom pretty much got out of my way and let me do my thing. After all, fencing became the connection between Dad and me. But that didn't mean she wasn't present for some of my greatest moments in the sport.

At the 1981 Michel Alaux NAC, I had my best result to date and placed second overall. (Unfortunately, my last bout ended at 2:15 a.m., so both Mom and Dad were already at home, in bed, sleeping.)

The pressure at these national point events was always immense, and, quite frankly, I wasn't that comfortable having my parents in the stands watching me compete.

I never, ever shaved on game day. I liked to look a little grungy and ornery, and besides, my fencing mask would irritate my face if I shaved before a day of fencing. But Mom, true to her mantra of always displaying good manners and always leaving the house looking presentable ("You never know who you might run into," she constantly remarked), came up to me during a break in the competition and said, in her inimitable Slovak accent, "Jeffrey, darling, vy didn't you shave today?"

She was dead serious, and I didn't know whether to laugh or cry. My Fencers Club teammates who were sitting next to me at the time certainly did, as they were crying *from* their laughter! For the next fifteen years, Eric Rosenberg would come up to me at every fencing competition and remark in his best Alice Bukantz voice, "Jeffrey, darling, you fat bum, vy didn't you shave today?"

Thanks, Mom!

But she wasn't finished with me yet. I was using a fencing mask made by a company called Prieur. Their masks were structured to be shallow in the front, which created a problem as my nose would never be described as shallow. My big nose rubbed against the steel mesh and caused me to look quite a bit like Rudolph the Red-Nosed Reindeer.

While I was still bristling over the shaving comment, Mom again approached me to offer her two cents. "Jeffrey, darling," she started, "that mask is rubbing against your nose and irritating it. Please let me buy you a new von, any von that you vant, okay?"

At that point, despite her good intentions, I felt like Popeye reaching for the spinach before saying, "I can takes all I can takes, but I can't takes no more!"

I looked at her incredulously, and just like Jackie Gleason's famous character Ralph Kramden used to shout to Art Carney's Ed Norton on *The Honeymooners*, I pointed to the exit door and shouted, "You, out!"

Perhaps that anger was harnessed and then channeled in the right direction because I went on to have the best tournament I'd ever had at the time. That was your plan all along, right Mom?

When I made the finals of the 1982 Cherry Blossom NAC in Fairfax, Virginia, Mom was there.

When I took fourth place at the 1986 US Nationals at Manhattan College, Mom was there.

When I earned a spot on the 1987 Pan American Games

Team at the Phoenix, Arizona National Championships, Mom was there.

When I marched into the Indianapolis Speedway with the United States Team at the Opening Ceremonies of the 1987 Pan Am Games, Mom was there.

When I refereed the finals of the 1996 Olympic Games in Atlanta, Mom was there.

But, what really mattered was that whenever I was down in the dumps and needed moral support, Mom was always there. She is the most selfless and giving person I've ever known.

Unfortunately, I've also had a pretty turbulent relationship with my mom. Let's just say that we are both stubborn and headstrong, and I've probably acted like a petulant child for the better part of our relationship.

Anyway, I had an epiphany in 1993 when I saw the movie *Schindler's List*. While Mom had never burdened me with stories about her terrible experience during the Holocaust, when I saw this film the reality of it all hit me over the head. I cried like a baby. I cried because of the overwhelming anger I had for the Nazis who tried to ruin my family. I cried because of the sorrow I felt for Mom and her parents and siblings. But I cried mostly because I realized how terribly I'd been treating my mom over the years.

When I saw her a few days later, I mustered up all my courage, got a little choked up, and said, "Mom, I promise to treat you nicely for the rest of our lives together."

Without any hesitation whatsoever, Mom riposted, "Oh, Jeffrey, darling, I only vish you had seen that movie fifteen years ago!"

Of course, Mom, if you dare vote for Hillary Clinton in 2008, all bets are off!

16

Jeff
the Ref

When I first started competing, Dad made two suggestions: Don't fence above your level, and get into refereeing. In 1974, though, I did exactly what he told me not to do, which was entering myself in the open competitions in New York. These tournaments were loaded with the best local fencers, some of whom were already Olympians. Dad felt that I should first succeed against my peers and not risk developing a "loser's" attitude when I inevitably got my big butt kicked by the much more experienced fencers. And he was right. In some of these early competitions, I was eliminated in the very first round, thereby proving his theory that I simply wasn't ready for this advanced level of competition.

After my early eliminations I had two choices: go home with my tail between my legs or stay and referee. He reasoned that becoming a competent referee would allow me to stay in the sport long after my active fencing days were over. I don't know why I ended up following Dad's second suggestion, but it turned out to be one of the best decisions I ever made. I stuck around after my eliminations to ref for as long as they would let me.

It became quite apparent that I wasn't ready to referee at this level any more than I was ready to fence at it. The same guys who clobbered me during the first round were now destroying me in the second round, albeit while I was refereeing to the best of my novice ability. It wasn't pleasant. I must have had some masochistic tendencies, that's for sure.

But I persevered through the verbal abuse. I learned from my mistakes and took heed of the fencers' "constructive" criticisms. Eventually, the same fencers who were yelling and screaming at my calls were requesting that I officiate the finals. I would rather have been fencing in the finals, but refereeing them was better than nothing.

And I enjoyed refereeing. For some, it provides an opportunity for a power trip, as the ref is the person in charge. For me, however, it was just another form of competition. I wanted my calls to be perfect; I wanted to be the best referee. And, true to form, I wanted to be like my dad, who was considered the best referee in the country and one of the best in the entire world. And thus another opportunity to follow in Danny Bukantz's impressive footsteps presented itself. Naturally, these weren't normal-sized footsteps; they were size 16 EEE, as he'd refereed the finals of multiple Olympic Games. Just being a decent American referee wouldn't cut it for Danny Bukantz's son. I'd also have to become the best ref in the country, as well as one of the best in the world. But, of course, I'd have to start small.

I cut my teeth at New York City high school competitions. It was fun, I made a few bucks, and it was the perfect place to learn, as my mistakes wouldn't matter too much.

I also continued to officiate at the local open tournaments. It wasn't unusual for me to compete on Saturday and take the train back into the city on Sunday at 8 a.m. to referee a women's competition. And yes, the women yelled at me, too! Most American fencers are familiar with Sharon Everson, referee and member of the USFA's Fencing Officials Commission. Sharon is a stickler who takes no guff from anyone. Just remember that she used to be… Sharon DiBiase! Thirty years later, I still have unpleasant flashbacks to a bout between Sheila Armstrong and Sharon DiBiase. Armstrong was a two hundred-pound Olympian with the best hand I've ever seen. And she had a temper as big as her frame. DiBiase's temper was infamous, as she was known for throwing her foils and mask while practicing at Salle Csiszar in Philadelphia. These two firebrands really gave me the business. I think they wanted to kill me.

But, as the saying goes, "If it doesn't kill you, it will only make you stronger." Thank you, Sheila and Sharon. You forced me to become stronger… a lot stronger.

After a few months I really started to get the hang of it and liked refereeing a lot. The fencers were starting to like me, which doesn't happen to bad referees. Actually, gaining approval from fencers isn't a regular occurrence for the good referees, either.

I was ready to take my next big step: college-level refereeing. Within a year of getting my name out there as an available referee, I was hired on a regular basis by Hunter, Hofstra, CCNY, NYU, St. John's, Barnard, Penn State, Pace, Pratt, and Baruch College. I became known as the best young referee in the area, and was in big demand.

At the same time, I was finally breaking through as a fencer; my schedule was full of fencing. Very few, if any, active fencers took officiating as seriously as I did. I dove in headfirst because I was driven to become the best referee in the country. I was living day-to-day in a crazed state. I was fencing. I was refereeing. I was fencing. And then I was refereeing some more.

In the winter of 1977 I officiated a quad meet at CCNY in Manhattan that started at 4:30 p.m. on a Friday and ended at 9:30 p.m. that night. I refereed the entire time, spending five hours straight on my feet. Then, as the snow began to fall in the city, I got into my car and spent another five hours driving through blizzard-like conditions to get to Penn State, where I'd be refereeing yet another quad meet at 8 a.m. sharp!

It was a crazy time, and sometimes I felt like I was going crazy. But I was actually crazy like a fox. The collegiate competitions I refereed were mostly girls' meets, and I was happily meeting my share of 'em. (I've since learned that dating the girls you refereed represented a conflict of interest, but it seemed perfectly reasonable at the time.)

After a loaded collegiate season in 1978, I 'rewarded' myself by flying out to Kenosha, Wisconsin to attend the NCAA Championships at the University of Wisconsin at Parkside. I arrived as a spectator, but offered my services as a referee. I was not only asked to referee, but assigned to all three weapons: foil, epee, and saber. I not only officiated all three weapons, but was also assigned to the gold medal bouts in both men's foil and epee.

At the age of twenty-one I was put in the position of officiating the most crucial bouts at my first NCAA tournament. The coaches loved my work, and the fencers, mostly around my age, accepted me immediately.

Only a couple referees were actually flown to Wisconsin by the NCAA. I paid my way, and I didn't receive an honorarium or per diem for four days of hard work on the strip. So, characteristically never short of *chutzpah*, I went right up to Wisconsin coach Loran Hein and asked if he could "take care of me" in the way of some financial reimbursement. He said he'd see what he could do.

I'll never forget when Coach Hein walked up to me the next day with a big smile on his face, shook my hand, and slipped me a twenty-dollar bill. Ha! I was happy to do it for free; even after airfare, lodging, and food, I was happy to pay to just be there. But twenty bucks?

My success at the NCAA tournament in Wisconsin had a dual effect. My confidence was through the roof, and I gained the respect of the fencing community as a top-notch referee. I couldn't put a price tag on that! (But seriously, twenty bucks?)

Since then I've officiated at nearly every NCAA Championship, and, in 2005, I was named Head Referee. I've always taken special pride in providing the best possible refereeing for these young adults. There is something so pure about the unbridled team spirit exhibited at the college level, and I wanted to enhance it by giving the fencers the best possible environment in which to compete.

My refereeing prowess was acknowledged throughout the fencing community; if I was eliminated from a national event before the finals, I'd be asked to shower, put on a jacket, and come back to the strip to officiate. I would much rather have been fencing the finals, but refereeing them was quite an honor, and it proved that I was now considered an elite national referee.

In 1980, when I was just twenty-three, I was assigned to officiate my first National Championship final. I was clearly one of the emerging top dogs, and my reputation as a competent referee was blossoming.

In 1981 and 1982 I ended up sixth in the foil point standings and at the same time was earning the reputation of becoming the best foil referee in the United States.

I figured it was time to try to take the jump into the international refereeing community.

* * *

To become an international referee I had to obtain my FIE (International Fencing Federation) referee's license, which involved taking both practical and oral examinations. My exams were set to happen in the spring of 1982 at the Cherry Blossom NAC in Fairfax, Virginia.

Guido Malacarne, an Italian and good friend of my parents, was set to proctor the tests. To nudge things in my good favor, my folks took Malacarne out for dinner prior to my exams.

The practical exam went off without a hitch, as I had expected. After all, I could ref with the best of them. The oral exam was a different story. I was ill-prepared for the rules questions Malacarne peppered me with. The questions were nit-picky and obscure, but even if they'd been plain vanilla, I still would have been in trouble. The fact is that I didn't study the rules thoroughly enough. I failed miserably.

Ralph Zimmermann, one of the international referees, once told me what Malacarne told him after I bombed the oral exam: "I was embarrassed for the father."

Well I know I embarrassed myself, that's for sure. But it was a life lesson, and I knew I'd get a second chance.

And that chance presented itself one year later at the World Championships in Vienna, Austria. I'd made the team – my first World Team! – but I also planned to retake the FIE referee test on a day I wasn't competing. I was determined to learn the rules and memorize the damn rulebook. I wasn't going to allow history to repeat itself in Vienna.

Leading up to the summer of 1983, my wife Carol (we were married on May 16, 1982) helped me with the process. She painstakingly tested me until we were both blue in the face. I knew the rules cold. Carol tested me so often that I'm convinced she could have passed the oral exam herself – probably with a higher score.

In Vienna the oral exam was to be administered by another friend of my parents, Dr. Rudolph Karpati, a Hungarian. I learned the hard way that friendship wouldn't get me anywhere from my first attempt at a referee's license. I was very nervous. Before the test my palms were as sweaty as when I'm in an airplane about to take off. Fortunately, my second stab at the exams experienced no turbulence whatsoever. Thanks to the countless hours of hard work and ceaseless efforts on behalf of Carol, I aced the exams and earned my FIE license. I was an officially licensed international referee!

I think Dad was happier than I was.

I was on my way to worldwide greatness. I was on my way to following in Dad's footsteps as a referee at the Olympic Games. I had arrived at the Big Show. I was as good as any foil referee in the world, and I was determined to continue the great Bukantz name.

After narrowly missing the Olympic Team in 1984, I was selected to go to Los Angeles as an extra referee. Dad was a Head Referee at these Games, his ninth consecutive (excluding the 1980 Moscow boycott). I was smart enough to realize I wasn't going to match that particular record; sometimes you just have to say, "Screw the footsteps!"

Though in Los Angeles I was primarily a side judge assisting the referees, Dad's name and position helped me grab an unprecedented assignment in the men's foil preliminary round. This level of refereeing was considerably more stressful than anything I had experienced previously, but I was told I did a perfect job in my initial Olympic outing.

My refereeing contributions at Los Angeles were merely the appetizer. I wanted to be the main course at the next Olympic Games in 1988 (that is, if I didn't make the US team as a competitor).

Initially, I was coming up in the fencing world as the next big American referee. I had friends in high places. Chaba Pallaghy was a big shot in both the US and FIE refereeing circles, and he was also one of Dad's best friends, a fact that was sure to help pave my way. But I couldn't expect Chaba to help me out unless I took care of my end of the deal: earning a stellar international reputation.

Chaba probably had a hand in my next major refereeing accomplishment. In 1985 I was assigned as the US referee at the 1985 Junior World Championships in Arnhem, Holland.

At the time, it was unheard of for a top-ranked fencer to become a top-ranked referee concurrently, but Danny Bukantz's son had some major footsteps to fill.

I stepped off the KLM flight in Amsterdam and, after retrieving my bags, expected to be met by someone to take me the rest of the way to Arnhem. Before departing the US, nobody had given me any instructions; I didn't even know what hotel the US team was staying at. All I was given by the USFA was my plane ticket!

I arrived on the scene as a big shot international referee, but nobody at the Amsterdam airport seemed to care. I broke out into my usual cartoon-character sweat at the thought of not even knowing where I was going in this country! I was totally drenched. For a brief moment, I entertained the thought of going to the KLM counter and booking the next flight right back to New York.

But then I remembered that an international referee such as myself must be able to stay calm under the most trying circumstances. So I decided to stick it out and find my way to Arnhem. How about that for good judgment?

I found a train going to Arnhem. I bought a ticket and off I went. But, I really had no idea where I was heading. My luck finally changed when I spotted a fencing bag in my train car. Our bags are easy to spot; they look like a golf bag. The bag's owner was Arnhem-bound too. Only one problem: I still had no idea what hotel to go to.

Then it came to me. My best chance at finding the US team hotel would be to find the US team. The best way to find the US team would be at the actual fencing site, where they'd – hopefully – be practicing. Fortunately, the young fencer on the train gave me the name and address of the fencing hall, so I had a chance.

After an all-night flight, a long train ride, and a jaunt about town in a taxi, I finally arrived at the site. I was unshaven, probably a little rank (actually, a lot rank after my flop sweat at the airport!), tired, rumpled, and very cranky. Basically, I walked into the fencing hall with a bad attitude.

But all of the negativity vanished instantly when I ran into the American fencers immediately upon entering the hall. I was finally able to find out where I'd be sleeping that night. Of course, the team had just started training and wouldn't be going back for a few hours, so I found a nice quiet nook, put my sweaty head on my tote bag, and fell asleep to the clinking of steel.

That was my indoctrination to the world scene. And, the tough part, the officiating, had yet to begin!

For the event, I was assigned to men's foil all the way until the last direct elimination bout prior to the finals. The refereeing was a piece of cake, and I seemed to be accepted into the international fraternity of referees without a hitch. The only real change was speaking in French, which is the language of the fencing. Learning to make the calls in French wasn't that tough; it only got hairy when a coach started arguing with me. I wouldn't understand most of what he was saying – or yelling – and I didn't have the ability to respond with my sharp English-only tongue. In these situations I just waved the coach back to the sideline with the back of my hand. Whenever a coach got in my face over a call, my propensity to perspire when nervous surfaced. I couldn't help it. That's just how my system reacts to stress. But the key for a referee when the going gets tough is to act like a duck.

A duck? Yup! No matter hard and fast a duck paddles under the water, it appears to be perfectly calm and under control on the surface. So, when fencers, coaches, and captains started quacking at me in a language I barely understood and the flop sweat started, I had to smile, make believe I was calm, and proceed to the next action.

I returned from Arnhem confident in myself and assured that I was on the fast track to greater heights; I was on my way to refereeing the Olympics in 1988!

And it only got better in 1986, at least from a refereeing standpoint. I was assigned to my second Junior Worlds held in Stuttgart, Germany. However, whereas I was a stud in Arnhem, I was a dud in Stuttgart. I wasn't given an assignment past the first round of the foil events. This was my first refereeing reality check and it was a definite blow. I kept wondering if the way I was assigned in Arnhem would prove to be the norm, or would it be the exception?

A few months after returning home from that disappointing stint in Germany, I just missed the World Championship team by two spots, although I had a very good competitive season. Though I missed the team, I was selected to represent the United States in Sofia, Bulgaria as the referee. Again, I posed a dual threat as both fencer and official, which was just so unprecedented at the time.

I was hoping to receive better treatment in Bulgaria than I did in Stuttgart. I was chomping at the bit for some serious refereeing action. But, as I had feared, I wasn't assigned past the preliminary rounds of the men's foil. Evidently, the FIE assignor in Bulgaria went with the referees he knew, and I was still a relatively new face.

I sensed a pattern developing. And it was beginning to become a little disheartening.

The only high points in Bulgaria were my assignments in the other weapons in addition to foil. I refereed men's saber, the toughest event to officiate and most definitely not my specialty. I was also assigned to men's epee, so at least there was a chance that my stock would rise as a three-weapon referee.

I had a major scare during the first round of epee and had to be very light on my feet. Of course, the snafu didn't happen on a side strip, but rather on the raised finals strip in the middle of the room where most of the spectators were looking. Basically, there were enough people around and enough people watching that I would be scrutinized for how I handled this brouhaha.

It happened during a bout between a Cuban fencer and a Swiss fencer. On one action, the Cuban attacked, but his point appeared to be a foot or so away from the Swiss. But his light, which signified a touch, appeared on the machine. Without hesitation, the Swiss fencer started jumping up and down and screamed – in French – something to me that I (luckily) was able to comprehend, *"No, monsieur, ne pas possible!"*

And he was right; what had happened was not possible. So I immediately called over the FIE Technician, Goran Abrahamson of Sweden (naturally, a friend of Dad's), and he took the Cuban's epee to inspect it and determine if it had been somehow rigged to register a phantom touch.

While Goran was back in the tech room, I walked by the Cuban, who was now sitting on the raised fencing strip waiting for the outcome. For the rest of my life, I will never forget what transpired next.

The Cuban, with bloodshot, albeit yellowish eyes, asked me in a broken combination of Spanish and French, *"Monsieur, c'est une problema 'grande' au 'poco'?"*

At that moment I knew he was cooked. "Was this a big problem or little?" Well, my friend, if you cheated, I think you already know the answer!

Goran returned after about twenty minutes, but it seemed to be an eternity. He showed me how the Cuban's epee had been rigged by taking the rubber tubing off the two wires inside the bell of the weapon. By doing this, the fencer could then, with a well-timed movement of his thumb, push the two un-insulated wires together, which would complete the electrical circuit. This would cause the light to register on the scoring machine as if he had scored a valid touch.

Unfortunately for this Cuban, he pulled the trigger when he was too far away from the Swiss fencer, and it alerted everyone that something was wrong. His devious jig was up.

But, I wasn't out of the woods quite yet. The FIE representative in charge of the competition came up to me with

146 Jeff the Ref

the rulebook and told me I had to make a choice. And though the rulebook was in French, I understood my options.

I had to determine whether the Cuban fencer would receive a black card and thus be expelled from just the day's competition or from the entire World Championships. If I chose the latter, it would mean from the epee team event, as well.

While it was entirely up to me, this FIE muckety-muck was testing me. This situation had become a litmus test to see what I was made of. At least, that's what I was told later that week by an official from the FIE.

If the Cuban had simply cursed me off, or something minor to that effect, it wouldn't have warranted an exclusion from the whole World Championship, but just that day's event. I immediately reasoned that cheating is the worst offense against the sport, and I would exclude the Cuban from the entire World tournament.

The FIE official smiled at me and said, "Good choice."

Whew! And that was during an epee bout, no less. Epee is the weapon with virtually no subjectivity at all. The referee is basically a police officer who enforces the rules. It's said that a ref can daydream for ninety-five percent of an epee bout, but if you aren't attentive during the other five, you will be terribly embarrassed.

On that day, I was wide-awake at the right moment. Maybe I just got lucky. But as Branch Rickey, General Manager of the Brooklyn Dodgers responsible for breaking the color barrier by signing Jackie Robinson, once said, "Luck is the residue of design."

In other words, those who work hard often get lucky. Basically, all of the hard work and preparation I had done for any situation paid off on that near-fateful day in Bulgaria.

Overall, 1986 was bust for me internationally as a referee. After a brief appearance at the 1984 Olympics and a huge splash at the 1985 Junior Worlds, I was energized. After being selected to referee both the 1986 Junior and Senior Worlds, I was really pumped. But, after not getting much work at either, I was totally deflated.

Why wasn't I used more often? Did they think I wasn't up to the task? Did I screw up terribly and not know it? Was it because I was still a new face on the scene? Was it my lack of ability to speak French fluently?

These thoughts took up residence in my tortured mind. My peers already recognized me as the #1 foil referee in the country, but for some reason, I was a non-entity internationally.

Even though I was frustrated, I grudgingly forged ahead in 1987. I wasn't a quitter, not in competition or refereeing. I started repeating a new mantra, "I'll show 'em!"

*   *   *

That year, 1987, became my signature year. I was ranked fifth at the season's end and earned a spot on both the World Championship and Pan American Games teams. Making these two prestigious teams was akin to making the Olympics, just a year early.

Yippee! I'd finally made it.

In keeping with my atypical dual career, I was selected to officiate at my third consecutive Junior Worlds in 1987, which were being held in Sao Paolo, Brazil. The Junior Worlds were always held over Easter vacation, which generally coincided with the Jewish Passover holiday. So, for the third straight year, I spent Passover in a foreign country. By chance, my parents were hosting the Passover Seder in Forest Hills on the night I was to depart for Brazil; this would work out for me, as I was flying out of JFK, only fifteen minutes from their home.

One of the questions asked during the Passover Seder is, "Why is this night different from all other nights?"

Well, this night was really different. After leaving the Seder early to catch a taxi to the airport, there was another wrinkle to deal with. My favorite sports team, the New York Rangers, was playing its rival, the Philadelphia Flyers, in an important playoff game that night. For me, quite frankly, that game meant more to me than fencing or Jewish holiday traditions.

So here's what I did. I got to the airport with an hour and a half to spare before the flight. I called my dad and had him put the radio next to the receiver while he went back to the dinner table. So I was able to listen to the game. Let's just say that my palms were sweaty – and not even from anticipating the plane's takeoff this time.

The hockey game was in the third and final period with my beloved Rangers trailing the Flyers 3-2. The airport loudspeaker blared, "Final boarding call for Sao Paolo." I never left – and refused to leave – the pay phone.

Finally, an incredulous airline employee left her spot at the counter, came over to me, and said sternly, "Sir, if you don't get on the plane right now, we're leaving without you."

I boarded with five minutes left in the game, miserable because the Rangers were losing and even more miserable that I wouldn't know the outcome until we reached the bottom of the hemisphere sometime the next day.

The Rangers lost. It was an bad omen, because in Sao Paolo, so would I.

For my third consecutive Junior Worlds, I received no assignments past the preliminary rounds. I was devastated. And I was pissed.

I made up my mind then and there that I would not pursue the international refereeing scene just to be an early-round body, basically the cannon fodder of referees. Whereas I always had some doubts about my fencing abilities, I always had supreme confidence in my officiating prowess.

Why was I assigned to the NCAA gold medal bouts every year? Why was I assigned to national gold medal bouts in women's and men's foil when I didn't make the finals myself? For crying out loud! Why had I been selected for three straight Junior Worlds and a Senior Worlds if I wasn't the real deal?

I knew I was the real deal. I was as good as any foil referee on the planet, but I wasn't getting the international push. That push was going to rising star Russell Wilson. While Russell deserved a push, he didn't deserve to have his push completely overwhelm mine. But it did. Wilson was the new favorite son of both Chaba Pallaghy and Ralph Zimmerman.

His rising star was deserved, as Wilson was hungry, dedicated, and talented. Wilson's stock was further inflated by the fact that he was a saber ref, the hardest weapon to officiate. And another thing: Wilson spoke a few languages and embraced the political aspect of the international scene. Those interests sealed the deal. It was the opinion of Pallaghy and Zimmerman, the decision-makers at the time in the US, that Wilson would get the big push.

I chose to shy away from fencing politics and let my refereeing do the talking. Mine was a conscious choice, and one I stood by. Yup — I stood by it while Wilson passed me by.

For the record, Wilson and I were, and remain, great friends. He understood my dilemma and was sympathetic to my situation. We roomed together on the international trips; there was no antipathy whatsoever. It was just unfortunate that Wilson's glory was ruining my story.

Sadly, I only missed the 1988 Olympic Team by three spots. I was always close to the top five during the '80s, but the competition was fierce. Mike Marx, Greg Massialas, and Peter Lewison were far and away the best fencers around, and they locked up three of the five spots every year. Then, there would be ten or more guys like me fighting and clawing for the remaining two openings. I'm proud to have grabbed one of those spots a few times, albeit not during an Olympic year.

While I was downtrodden on the subject of international refereeing, I was again selected as a referee for the 1988 Junior Worlds, my fourth consecutive year. That year's events took place at the University of Notre Dame. While en route to South Bend, I was determined that the competition would be the final litmus test – both for me and those assigning me – as FIE representatives from the US would be making the assignments.

Best of all, I was assured that I would finally receive my push; I was basically promised at least one assignment in the finals, something that would make the last few years of frustration worthwhile. Once a referee succeeds in a World Championship final, he becomes "made" in the cliquish and closed world of international refereeing.

And one other great piece of news that year: Russell Wilson would not be attending. I had spoken to him on the phone the week leading up to the competition and he confirmed this.

Finally! The stars were beginning to align in my favor. The brass ring would be there for the taking, and there was no way I was leaving South Bend without it.

I had a promise from Ralph Zimmerman that I'd be used in the foil finals, and he was a man of his word. Chaba Pallaghy acknowledged that with Wilson out, I would be the fair-haired American referee. After three long years of shoddy treatment, my ship was about to come in. Unless lightning struck me down, I would leave the 1988 Junior Worlds as a respected world-class fencing referee, just like Dad.

I was ready. I knew it was time to put up or shut up. If I bombed, those who *didn't* assign me, for whatever reason, would be proven right. And, whatever self-esteem and self-confidence I had left would go right down the toilet.

* * *

The day before competition began, I found out that Wilson decided to attend after all. He apologized profusely, claiming that he was pressured to come by Zimmerman and Pallaghy. I sensed this was not a good omen, but I also felt that this was to be my Junior Worlds, not his. Besides, the powers-that-be had told me so themselves.

I actually ended up rooming with Zimmerman in South

Bend, which was really terrible luck, as he was a world-class snorer. Sure enough, on the eve of my big day, the men's foil finals, Zimmerman came into the room around midnight, fell dead asleep, and immediately started sawing wood. It was brutal.

I tossed and turned for almost two hours; I must have resembled a rotisserie chicken. I stuck my fingers in my ears, punched the wall; I tried everything. There was no way I even came close to falling asleep; the combination of Zimmerman's snoring and my being furious had my heart racing.

I decided to improvise. I took my pillow and comforter and went into the bathroom around 3 a.m. I laid down on the floor and curled myself around the toilet. After calming down, I actually fell asleep.

Hey, I reasoned, three hours of sleep would refresh me, and I would still be at the top of my game the next morning.

At around 5 a.m., I was rudely awakened from of a deep sleep by a loud knocking on the bathroom door. Ralphie-boy had to pee, and that was the end of my sleeping for the night. The entire ordeal was a nightmare; ironically I was awake for most of it.

But the finish line was in sight, and nothing would deter me from a peak performance in the men's foil finals the next day – my big day!

Only the slightest bit bleary-eyed, I made my way to the fencing hall in the morning. As per usual, while the other refs were drinking coffee or just chilling, I was warming up. It was my schtick: I had to warm up my eyes by watching fifteen to twenty minutes of the fencers as they practiced. I would make sure to move around the hall so that I could see as many fencers and different styles as possible.

Other refs laughed at my warm-up ritual. But, I'd rather have refs laughing at me beforehand than having fencers and coaches yelling at me if I came in "cold" and made a few early mistakes because I *hadn't* warmed up!

Early on in the day, I was assigned to the first round in the men's foil. No problems; no arguments. It was smooth sailing.

And, while I held my breath as the loudspeaker called the names of the assigned referees for subsequent rounds, my own would not be called again that day. Not during the next two rounds of pools and not once for direct elimination.

I stewed in silence. While tempted to go up to Zimmerman or Pallaghy, who were involved in making the assignments, to ask them what was going on, I was steadfast not to. I was the proud son of Dr. Daniel Bukantz. I wanted to make my own name as a referee. I wasn't going to ride into the international scene on his famous coattails nor beg for the assignments I wanted and deserved.

I stewed all day. And the stewing only intensified when my good buddy Russell Wilson received an assignment in the men's foil finals that night. Though frustrated, I rooted for him to do well. I was sincerely and honestly very happy for Russell. But I was throwing my very own pity party. Danny Bukantz's son was sad, angry, and disillusioned. My emotions that day were raging, and I knew that my last chance would be in the women's foil, still two days away.

With or without Zimmerman's snoring, it was going to be another rough night of sleep.

I was probably assigned to some saber or epee the next day, but I don't remember. My focus was on the following day.

After the mistreatment in the men's foil, I started having rightful doubts about whether Zimmerman and Pallaghy would fulfill their promise to use me in a final at this competition. But, I still had to take them at their word, and that's what (barely) kept my spirits up as I arrived in the fencing hall at 7:30 a.m. for the women's foil event. This was to be the biggest day of my refereeing career, and I was ready, albeit a bit nervous.

When I wasn't assigned to the first round of pools I merely thought, "Hmm, that was weird." Maybe it was luck of the draw; maybe they were intentionally saving me with the plan to use me all day through the finals.

As the second round assignments came over the public address system, I held my breath. I breathed a sigh of relief after my name was called. Whew! Okay, time to go to work. Time to do what I do as well as anyone in the world. Time to make the FIE people see that there's a new Bukantz in town.

As per usual, the pool went by without any problems. It was time for the direct elimination rounds – the longer knockout bouts that had all the visibility and the added pressure that went with them.

I held my breath as the refs for the top thirty-two were announced. But... my name was not among them.

I held my breath while the refs for the top sixteen were announced. Again, my name was missing.

The refs for the top eight were announced. I held my breath. Nothing.

The refs for the *repecharge* (loser's) bracket were called. I held my breath, but to no avail.

It seemed as if I'd been holding my breath for most of that three-hour timeframe. I probably could have tried out for a synchronized swimming team after holding my breath for that long!

Something was badly out of sync. It was my psyche. For the second consecutive foil event, I was relegated to a scrub, a ref only assigned to a single preliminary round. For the third consecutive Junior World Championships, I hadn't been assigned to even one direct elimination bout.

It was clear to me on that sad day in April 1988 that I'd failed to make the grade as a top-notch international referee. And, what made it even harder to accept was that, for once, I was not concerned about filling Dad's footsteps. I was looking to fill my own!

But it was not to be.

How I went from the best referee in the United States to a

bum internationally is hard to explain. However, on that fateful day, it was no longer about footsteps. It was about personal pride. And my pride could take no more.

So, as I sat despondent in the stands with my old friend Matt Harris, I made a decision that didn't come easily; but once my mind was made up, there was no turning back. I said to Harris, "Matt, I'm about to throw away my entire international refereeing career. This isn't a snap judgment, but rather something that has been brewing for three years. The time is right. I made a pact with myself never to subject myself to this if I didn't get a fair chance to fail or succeed. I promised myself I wouldn't stay in it as a first-round bum. So, watch this."

I got up and went down a few steps to the fencing floor. I walked right over to Zimmerman and Pallaghy and, without any anger, calmly told them, "Guys, I love you and appreciate everything you've done for me. However, you promised I'd finally get my chance here, and you didn't come through."

"Thanks for everything," I continued, "but I quit. I'm out of here."

Pallaghy, without a second's hesitation, responded loudly as I was walking away, "Bukantz, you're making a big mistake!"

I responded by continuing to walk away.

I went back to Harris; we got up, left the facility, and went out to get drunk.

In a show of complete insubordination, which the FIE wasn't accustomed to, I didn't come to the site the next morning. Of course, I'd been assigned to the first round of men's epee.

Just like that, I closed the door on my international refereeing career.

But you know what? I didn't have any second thoughts. Not for one second did I feel I made the wrong decision. There was something so right about what I chose to do, how I did it, and when I did it.

I walked away with my head held high. I resigned myself to continue and enjoy officiating in the US, where I was appreciated and respected. I would ref what I enjoyed, which was collegiate meets and national events. I'd go back to being a superstar and never look back at this frustrating and sad chapter of my life.

I would hold my breath no longer.

* * *

Postscript

A few months after my abrupt resignation, I received a call from Dad. He said Chaba was at the office to have his teeth worked on. And, finally, I got the answer to all of the questions as to what possibly could have held me back.

"Jeff," Dad said, "Chaba says you don't play the game enough. You don't get involved in the international social and political scene enough."

Although this call took place nearly two decades ago, I remember my response vividly.

"Dad, this is the way I see it," I replied, "I fly around the world and see nothing but the fencing gym, the airplane, and the hotel. I spend an inordinate amount of time away from my family. I spend an inordinate amount of time away from work, which costs me thousands of dollars."

I continued without coming up for air. "When I walk into the fencing hall each day I start off as perfect, and when I leave each day I'm accused of being either incompetent or unscrupulous. And, for this great opportunity, I have to kiss someone's ass in a language I don't even speak? Please tell Chaba I still love and respect him, but I'm not playing. Talk to you tomorrow when I cool down."

So, even if I was given a reprieve for my actions at South Bend, I made sure to let the person who controlled my international refereeing destiny know that my career was officially over.

17

The Dr. D Open

The top local competitions, as mentioned previously, were the Metropolitan Division's New York "Opens." The Opens separated the men from the boys, the contenders from the pretenders, the wheat from the chaff… While points and national rankings weren't at stake, any top fencer worth his or her salt would attend nearly every Metropolitan Division Open, most of which were held at the New York Fencers Club. Doing well at an Open was a serious matter to all involved, as personal pride was always a factor. The Opens were a barometer to see where a fencer stood in the pecking order and a way to determine who the strongest fencers, both physically and mentally, were.

A fencer's result at an Open was the indicator that revealed if all the lessons, practicing, footwork, and sparring had paid dividends. There was nothing better than strutting into the club on the first night of practice after a successful Open; on the contrary, there was nothing worse than shuffling into the club after bombing out at an Open. These competitions were like periodic tests to see if you had learned the material.

There was a men's foil Open pretty much once a month. Medals were awarded to the eight finalists. The Open and its medals were named after a renowned local fencer, and the medals were engraved accordingly.

Quite frankly, not many – if any – fencers cared about the name on the medal – their only concern was in what place they finished. And that was perfectly normal. Why would anyone care whose Open it was anyway?

Well, no other fencer was Danny Bukantz's son. And, of course, one of the annual Opens was the Dr. Daniel Bukantz Open.

On my schedule of competitions, I affectionately referred to this one as the "Dr. D Open."

Trying to match any of Dad's impressive accomplishments was nearly impossible. The toughest part of any attempt usually involved winning something big, be it a spot on a national or international team, refereeing at an international event, or bringing home Maccabiah gold. But Dad obviously never won the Dr. Daniel Bukantz Open because competitions weren't named for fencers until after they stopped competing.

While there wasn't anything to duplicate – for once – I had a burning desire to win my Dad's Open. It would mean the world to me. Any medal from Dad's tournament would have been nice, but the gold medal would have been the ultimate feather in my cap.

I was a really tough competitor. The combination of loving to win and hating to lose tended to make me a little crazed on the strip. Add the big, fat chip on my shoulder from needing to follow in my dad's footsteps and you were left with what the *Los Angeles Times* called, "the John McEnroe of Fencing."

The late Fred Shero, while he was the coach of the Stanley Cup Champion Philadelphia Flyers, wrote one of his typically cryptic inspirational phrases on the locker room blackboard: "Arrive at the puck in ill humor."

In other words, two guys go for the same puck in the corner; one comes out of that corner with the puck. You be the guy.

Well, while I hated the Flyers – or as we in New York called them, the Broad Street Bullies – I loved Shero's thinking. My philosophy when fencing was similar: two guys arrive on the strip and one leaves the winner. It may as well be me.

So I always arrived at the strip in ill humor. And it usually worked!

When competing in the Dr. D Open, ill humor was the understatement of all time. This was my dad's medal and you better believe I was out for blood. The Open presented an interesting contrast; while no other fencer cared one iota about the name on the medal, that alone exponentially increased my intensity. I was usually a wild animal in competitions; at the Dr. D Open I was rabid. I'm sure that I must have foamed at the mouth a few times during this particular competition.

One such occurrence took place during the 1986 Dr. D Open. In the semi-final bout – the round of four – I was fencing Steve Gross, who was a teammate of Eric Rosenberg and Mitch Dorfman from that 1972 Cardozo High School team. (Wasn't that the team that just wouldn't go away?)

Gross was an incredibly annoying person to fence. His style was annoying. His incessant complaining was annoying. His personal mannerisms were annoying. It was even annoying when his wife used to browbeat him in front of everyone.

The match-up between Mr. Annoying and Mr. Ill Humor had World Wrestling Federation pay-per-view potential. This bloodbath even required a special guest referee to handle matters. This referee was none other than my clubmate Nat 'The Hawk' Cohen.

Nat's a really great guy and a really good fencer – but he's blind in one eye. And, yes, it happened in a fencing accident. Once during a bout, after Nat scored a touch, his opponent, who was trying to show the referee why the call should have gone his way, made a move with his blade to demonstrate his version of what had happened. Unbeknownst to this fencer, Nat had already taken off his mask to shake the opponent's hand. And, in an accident we'll never forget, my good buddy Nat permanently lost his sight in one eye. Tragic.

That Nat was able to do all of that reading at Yale and at med school is a testament to him. That even with the loss of depth perception he would become one of the best fencers in the country is beyond me.

As a competitor, Gross was also tough as nails. It was a challenge to fence against him not only because he was good, but because he also had a way of throwing you off your game as you tried to take his head off. But, in our 1986 match-up, he was up against The Master.

In the ten-touch bout, Gross was leading 4-3. On my next action, I reverted to Ol' Faithful: the counter-four parry and riposte. It was a classic move. A textbook move – and it had worked, or so I thought. Thinking I had tied the score, I let loose a war whoop right in Gross's annoying face. Poor Nat must have watched the action with his bad eye; he gave the touch to Gross. I was as mad as I've ever been. Instead of tying the score at 4-4, I was now down by two. I wasn't upset at Nat; he'd made an honest mistake. But I was furious at Gross.

I looked Gross right in the eye and said, "Why don't you acknowledge that touch? It was the nicest touch I scored all day! You know it was against you."

Gross, with that annoying face of his, just shrugged his shoulders and looked as if he was the cat that swallowed the canary. I pleadingly asked again, "You're not going to give me that touch?"

He just shrugged and got ready for the next action.

It's possible, right after I put my mask back on, that I really did start foaming at the mouth. Not that Mr. Ill Humor needed any extra incentive to get fired up, but his blatant lack of sportsmanship meant war.

During the following five minutes, Steve Gross received an ass-whooping he'll never forget. He had to pay. When we fenced in close quarters, I clobbered him with shoulders, elbows, forearms, knees – whatever I could clobber him with! When he tried to fleche past me, I sent him airborne with a hip check that would have made Fred Shero proud.

A shell-shocked Nat, who probably wanted to avoid incurring my wrath any further, let all of my offensives go. When I wasn't hitting Gross with various parts of my body, I was hitting him with my foil. I ran the table after Nat's bad call and outscored Gross 7-0 to win the bout 10-5.

I went on to win the Open shortly after a relatively easy bout against crafty veteran Maurice Kamhi, who had absolutely no chance against this manic buzz-saw.

I won the Dr. D gold medal, by the way.

Afterward, in the locker room, I approached Gross and asked him why he didn't have the sportsmanship to give me the obvious touch. His answer left me speechless.

"Jeff," he started, "I never earned my A rating, and if I beat you and then won this tournament, I would have gotten it."

I think even Mr. Annoying felt some remorse over his decision to not be a good sport. For a brief, fleeting moment even I felt bad for him.

But it passed and, in retrospect, I sure am glad that he did what he did, as it lit a fire under my ass. Come to think of it, he wouldn't have been a very fitting winner of the Dr. D Open.

Throughout my career I won hundreds of medals. Most of them looked exactly alike aside from their bronze, silver, or gold coloring. I put all of these medals into a display case that hangs on the wall of my basement fencing room.

But I kept all nine of the Dr. D Open medals separate from the rest. These nine medals are in a special display case, as they are my most treasured medals. This beautiful display case hangs on the wall of my old room at my folk's apartment in Forest Hills. My old room is now my dad's study. Under these nine medals there is a small gold plate with the following inscription: "Dr. Daniel Bukantz Open."

I competed in the Dr. D Open nine times and in the case are the nine medals I had won.

And on three occasions, Danny Bukantz's son won the Dr. D gold medal.

18

The John McEnroe of Fencing

Danny Bukantz is considered an even greater sportsman than a competitor, which really speaks volumes about his character. He has always been a gentleman on and off the fencing strip, and he has always carried himself with a calm demeanor and an air of dignity.

In this respect, the apple fell far – very far – from the family tree.

I carried myself with a big chip on my shoulder. I had a razor's edge, an acerbic tongue, and a hair-trigger temper. Hey – this following in my dad's footsteps stuff brought with it a lot of pressure. Maybe this was just my way of blowing off some of it.

Actually, I blew off a lot of steam as well as a lot of people in the fencing community. Even during committee meetings, I took no prisoners. As a sixteen-year (four-Olympic-quadrennials) member of the USFA's High Performance Committee, I was very strident when pursuing any issue I believed in. This approach had some short-term success, but in the long run it had the effect of alienating the other members.

My voice, I was told, was akin to fingernails on the chalkboard, and it turned people off. I learned the hard way that being correct or fighting for a good cause is never enough. If not presented in an engaging and appealing manner, my positions and ideas fell on deaf ears.

And I blew off, in a big way, almost every referee.

As a competitor, I chewed up referees and spit them back out. Of course, I knew how far I could push them and picked my battles accordingly. I was always very careful with the experienced refs; pushing their buttons – especially the wrong ones – had the risk of backfiring. Backfiring could mean the difference between a win and a loss. When the refs lost patience with me, they would lean on me during the bouts, not give me the close calls, or – heaven forbid – give me a black card. The black card, the worst penalty a fencer can receive, means immediate expulsion from the competition.

I never received a black card for dissing a referee; I was way too savvy for that.

But I did get one during my competitive career.

During an NAC in 1993, a fencer named MacKenzie from Canada beat me at my own game. I was the king of crazy antics. The wilder things got on the strip, the better I performed. It was weird; I actually thrived on the extracurricular activities – the mind games.

When it came to gamesmanship and schtick, nobody could hang with me. I would have been in a league of my own were it not for MacKenzie. Our bout became quite physical and the tension was thick. After one action, MacKenzie walked right up to me, got in my face, and said, "I'm going to cut you up like a turkey for Christmas dinner."

Instead of coming up with one of my quick and quip-witted comebacks, I freaked. As MacKenzie turned around to walk to his en garde line, I punched him in the back. I punched him so hard that he actually slid off the back of the fencing strip.

I just completely lost it. Those words – "cut you up" – must have sent me over the edge. To me, those words went beyond garden variety trash talk; they were a threat!

The referee, Francisco Martin, was stunned. Everyone watching the bout – and the crowd had grown as they sensed a potential brouhaha growing – was stunned. That punk MacKenzie, now laid out flat on his weasel ass, was stunned.

I was stunned.

It was the first time in my lengthy competitive career that someone had actually gotten under my skin. MacKenzie beat me at my own game, and I was in big trouble.

Martin, after the initial shock wore off, realized he had no choice but to give me a black card. It was the only "black" mark on my competitive fencing career.

At the very next NAC, serendipity allowed for a Bukantz-MacKenzie rematch in the first match of the day. My heart was still pounding as a result of his "cut you up" threat, but I was too crafty a veteran to let this jerk get the upper hand on me again.

I did what I had to do to gain revenge: I whooped him, 5-1. Cut that up, MacKenzie – you lowlife!

As a fencer, I was feared. Fencers and referees were always concerned that I was up to something. And that worked to my advantage – the same way it worked for Hall of Fame baseball player Gaylord Perry.

Who was Gaylord Perry? During his Hall of Fame career, Perry was best known and worst remembered for throwing an illegal pitch, the heinous spitball. A spitball would cause the ball to move in an abnormal and unexpected manner due to the friction the spit caused. Perry admitted to his transgressions in his autobiography. While he owned up to throwing the illegal pitch, he was quick to add: "It didn't matter if I was loading up the spitball. As long as the batters were always on edge that I was throwing it was enough. The reality is that I didn't throw it that often. They just thought I did."

In that respect, I was the Gaylord Perry of fencing. Fencers and referees were always worried that I was doing something provocative, whether complaining or initiating body contact – whatever I could manage to get away with.

As long as they were on edge, I had an edge.

In one specific area, I was accused of throwing the fencing spitball. On the strip, I used to sweat profusely. My fencing glove would soak through after just a couple bouts. I'd have to change my glove as many as five times during a long competition.

Now, when a fencer's glove becomes completely wet and he squeezes the grip on the metal foil handle, it could have the effect of grounding out the machine. In layman's terms: the opponent's light wouldn't register when a touch was scored. (New machines are now designed to protect against grounding out.)

It was a potential method of cheating. And, I was wrongly accused of having employed this tactic intentionally. Of course, that was *never* the case, but it kept my opponents on edge. And, to add to their concern, I made sure to let everyone know that I had marinated all of my fencing gloves the entire day before the competition.

I drove them crazy! And I laughed like crazy! With regard to their accusations, *they* were the ones who were all wet.

I was not a gentle and dainty fencer; I was a bruiser. My blade actions were hard and I lived for the physicality. Body contact, albeit illegal in fencing and warranting penalty cards, was my friend. Let's just say it worked to my advantage, as most fencers gave me a wide berth.

Yet some fencers failed to respect and fear my reputation and gave me no alternative but to teach them a lesson.

In the early '80s I was getting ready for the first round of an Open at the Fencers Club. There was a tremendous teenage fencer in my pool, Marc Kent. He was a nice kid, but his father, Joe, was an ex-patriot Englishman and a bit pompous.

Shortly before our bout, Marc and I happened to be standing next to one another. Joe came over and, in his snooty British accent, said, "Well, Marc, you've got your work cut out for you, but at least you'll have plenty of target to hit."

Okay, so I was a big boy. I'd taken craps bigger than Marc Kent. And no, I did not appreciate being crapped on by his father.

At the beginning of the bout, it was like Marc had been shot out of a cannon. He attacked and scored two quick touches before I even knew what had hit me. On the second one, he actually ran me into the radiator against the wall at the end of the strip; if not for that radiator, we might have landed on 71st Street.

Dum de dum dum.

On the next action, I knew the youngster would explode at me with another attack. This time, however, I wouldn't try to retreat and back away. Instead, I extended my blade with a "point-in-line" just before he started his advance. But Kent had so much momentum that it was too late for him to stop. He came at me at full speed and my point hit him to score the touch. As I had remained in place, Kent ran right into me and was met with a stiff forearm to the mask. The blow was sure to leave a mark on Marc.

Bingo. He took off his mask; his nose was clearly broken. Bent in half! And, to boot, I scored the touch on the action.

It was clear that the fencing strip was my domain. You entered at your own risk. It only got riskier if your father had the nerve to insult me. My nose was bent out of shape because of the rude remark, so I reciprocated. A nose for a nose.

For the record, Marc went on to win the NCAA foil championship in 1988. I was the referee for the gold medal bout. And I was the referee he wanted.

Although Marc, Joe, and I have shared a laugh or two over the years, I do regret breaking Marc's nose. I was just a big bully that day.

On another day, however, bully tactics were in order.

At yet another Open at the Fencers Club, I was fencing clubmate Dan Rainford. Rainford was built like Adonis and strong as an ox. His fencing style was wild, out of control, and potentially dangerous. Rainford's physicality was omnipresent and nobody wanted to fence him for fear of sustaining an injury. In fact, when sparring at the FC, and Rainford was 'on deck,' both fencers would try to lose on purpose so as not to have to fence Dangerous Dan.

I was The Master, but Rainford was The Brute. This match was destined to be another pay-per-view, no-holds-barred, last-man-standing slugfest.

Rainford had entered my domain, and it was time for him to feel some pain.

I waited patiently for my opportunity to crush him. I allowed him to get some shots in and he pummeled me with excessive body contact. It was a rope-a-dope, the same thing Muhammed Ali did to beat George Foreman in the 1974 "Rumble in the Jungle" in Zaire.

We were fencing on the strip where Csaba Elthes gave his lessons during the week. "Csaba's strip," as it was known, had two pillars on one of its sides. (You already know where this is going, don't you?) My NYAC buddy, Jim Bonacorda, was watching our bout intently because he would face the winner. And, I think he knew something was about to go down.

Finally, I allowed Rainford to push me down the strip, just about to the area where the pillar was on my left. I looked at Bonacorda, and, like Babe Ruth, called my shot. "Watch this, Jim," I muttered under my breath and through my mask.

As expected, Rainford fleched and attempted to pass me on the left. Big mistake. VERY big mistake. At the perfect moment, I shifted slightly to my left and hit him with the mother of all hip checks. Rainford hit the pillar with a resounding thud and crashed to the ground with a sickening splat. I'm not exaggerating when I tell you that he had the birds flying around his head, just like in the cartoons. He was gone.

Best of all, I was able to convince the referee that Rainford had actually run into me. So not only did The Brute get knocked silly, but he was also handed a yellow card for causing the body contact. Ha!

Long live The Master… of Disaster!

When competing in a NAC, the pressure was enormous. Fencers flew in from around the country and they were all looking for national points. Everyone was loaded for bear.

In an NAC in Portland, Oregon in 1989, I tied for my best result when I took second to Lewison. However, in the second round I was stuck in a killer pool that was stocked with top fencers. I was at great risk of being eliminated early on. To move onto the next round, I basically had to win three or four of six bouts.

My second bout in the pool would be against Mike Marx, the best fencer of the era. Knowing this, I also knew that there was no way I could afford to lose the first bout. Starting out in this brutally tough pool with a 0-2 record would be daunting.

In the first bout, my opponent and I went touch for touch until the score was 4-4. On the last action, referee Peter Burchard reversed the call and gave the touch and the win to my opponent. All I could think about was my next bout with Marx and how impossible a win against him seemed. To lose such an important bout on a bad call… and with Marx up next… I was livid.

And as I unhooked myself from the electrical reel wire that completes the scoring circuit, I lost it. I held the reel cord, which was insulated with bullet-proof Kevlar, brought it to my mouth, and chomped down as hard as I could.

I bit straight through the bulletproof Kevlar cord! I held the two frayed pieces in my hands for just a second before handing them off to the next fencer, Alan Weber. Weber was shocked. He looked at me with a combination of disbelief and awe and said, "Ah, Jeff! What did you go and do that for?"

It was a moment of temporary insanity, a moment that could result in a black card if the ref had seen me destroying equipment. So, after handing Weber the two pieces of reel cord, I quickly regained my senses. I bolted for the men's room, and hid there for a whole five minutes hoping that Burchard wouldn't find me or just forget about me while changing the reel.

And he did! Miraculously, Burchard just moved on to the next bout without hesitation. For the record, while I was still "reel"ing from losing the first bout on a bad call, I somehow regrouped to beat Marx in my next bout.

To this day, the cadre of armorers in the United States still talks about the day when Bukantz bit through the Kevlar reel cord! They always ask if I was worried about breaking my teeth. "Of course not," I always reply, "my dad's a dentist!"

And this dentist's son had no problem biting off the heads of administrators, opponents, referees – even the poor, innocent equipment.

* * *

In the pecking order in the world of fencing, the weaker fencers were known as "cannon fodder." I looked at referees in the same manner; if I spotted a weak one, I'd exploit that weakness to my advantage or blow the guy out of the water.

Danny Bukantz never thought or acted like that.

But I lived for the stuff. I loved needling the referees, and I never passed up an opportunity to do so.

Here's a classic moment I'm still proud of:

During a break at an NAC, I was at a restaurant with my Fencers Club teammates Jack Tichacek, Eric Rosenberg, Nat Cohen, and Jerome Demarque when a group of referees sat down at a table on the opposite side of the room. I called the waiter over and gave him five bucks to help us out with a small favor. The five of us deposited our eyeglasses onto his tray and he then delivered our offering to the referees' table.

They didn't "get it" right away, but in about the same amount of time it takes to decipher a tough action on the strip, they finally burst out laughing. Hey! At least they all got this call right!

Another example that perfectly illustrates my inability to deal with bad calls appropriately and avoid baiting the ref who makes them goes as follows:

During the 1989 Nationals in Orlando, I was 3-1 going into my last bout in the pools. However, due to the way the pool was playing out, I would have to win against Eric "Dr. Doom" Dew in order to make my way to the direct elimination round of thirty-two. The referee, Sharon Everson, made what I thought was a terrible call at the worst possible moment – a call that cost me the bout and eliminated me from the Nationals long before I was accustomed to leaving. (At the time, I was ranked #2 in the US.)

After the bout, I threw the single worst tantrum of my career. It was disgraceful and worthy of punishment. I was, admittedly, out of control, and the entire gym watched as I kicked equipment, threw clothes everywhere, punched the wall, and finally stomped out the seat cushion of the nearest, most unfortunate chair. It probably brought back memories for Everson from when she was Sharon DiBiase!

The typically no-nonsense Everson was stunned and let me go on my tirade for quite a while. But enough was enough; she finally came over to me and calmly and discreetly, but firmly, said, "Okay, Jeffrey, that's enough."

The next time I saw Sharon was at the Olympic Festival a month or so later. She was talking to George Kolombatovich, Gerrie Baumgart, and a group of referees near the Bout Committee table. Everyone in this group had heard about the incident; I could feel the air of apprehension as I approached their circle. Clearly, this was the moment to bury the hatchet once and for all, as the impact of my words would be magnified by the group setting.

I worked up the courage and went right up to Sharon. I put my arm around her shoulder and, with a look of humility and puppy-dog eyes, asked, "Sharon, have I ever formally apologized to you for the way I treated you at the Nationals?"

Sharon, evidently still smarting from the encounter with Mr. Hyde, brusquely replied, "No, Jeffrey, as a matter of fact, you haven't."

I sensed that the group of referees loved this piece of humble pie I appeared to be gagging on. But they knew they'd been had by a different type of "gag" when the ol' Bukantz smirk resurfaced as I looked at Sharon and, after the requisite pregnant pause, exclaimed, "Good!"

And then, of course, there's the situation that earned me my nickname: "The John McEnroe of Fencing."

During the men's foil team event at the 1984 Nationals in Chicago, referee David Ladyman of Texas had a shot to obtain a higher rating. He was given the unenviable task of presiding over the bout between the New York Fencers Club and our opponent in the round of eight. The assignor felt that if any referee could deal with the NYFC, then he or she really earned the higher rating.

It was to be the ultimate proving grounds. (For some, their final resting grounds.) A bout between anyone and the NYFC was always destined to be tumultuous. Ladyman, a decent enough referee, was in way over his head.

The *Los Angeles Times*, in anticipation for the 1984 Olympic Games, sent a reporter to cover the Nationals. The following was printed in the *Los Angeles Times* back in June 27, 1984:

> *"The pressure on men and women who officiate fencing bouts is great: to see and interpret the fast blade action and handle the pleas and complaints of the fencers with assured confidence.*
>
> *"It's a bit mean, but when persons seeking 'directing' credentials are being rated during a bout by established directors (referees), the fencers know it and add some more pressure of their*

own. Shades of John McEnroe on the tennis court.

"During one foil bout at the national championships, Jeffrey Bukantz of New York saw that his angry reaction to mistakes was steadily increasing the new director's anxiety.

"Michael McCahey, Bukantz's teammate, said Bukantz at one point took off his mask and made a monster-like grimace and shrieked in the face of the director.

"As the man started telling his reviewer, Al Davis, that he lost the action, Bukantz said, 'Going... going...'

"Davis asked if he needed him to go over the last touch. (Electronic scoring machines record touches, but a director has to say whether a touch was scored in a legitimate way.)

"'No, I've lost control,' he said with a dazed look, and turned and walked away from the fencing strip.

"'...gone,' Bukantz said."*

Poor Ladyman walked out of the gym and was not, to my knowledge, ever seen again at a national event.

Hey! McEnroe and I are both from Queens, New York. McEnroe and I are both left-handed. McEnroe and I both used intimidation tactics to our advantage. And, yes, McEnroe and I were both jerks. He certainly won more championships than I did, but he had nothing on me in the antics department.

Well, Dad, you did tell me to go out and make my own name in the sport...

---

*"During one foil at the national championships, Jeffrey Bukantz of New York..." by John Dart. Copyright, 1984, Los Angeles Times. Reprinted with permission.

19

A Father's Day to Remember

The 1985 season was somewhat disappointing. While the post-Olympic year is always an "off year," that wasn't the case for me. After all, I was on a mission to qualify for the 1985 US Maccabiah Team and win Dad's gold medal.

While I made the team, I only won the bronze medal. For most, that would have been a great accomplishment. To be frank, it was a great result for me too. But, getting the bronze fell short of matching Dad's result, so my effort at the Maccabiah Games in 1985 was ultimately a failure of sorts for me. There was no getting around it.

After returning from the Games in July, I decided I really needed a break from fencing. I had been training, competing, and traveling for about a decade; I was pretty much going nonstop.

There was so much pressure on me to succeed. Of course, one hundred percent of that pressure I had knowingly put on myself. And after a while the pressure starts getting to you. The pressure to train, the pressure to win, the pressure to stay ahead of your competitors – the ever-present pressure! The nagging injuries took their toll as well.

And as if I could forget, there was still all that pressure to follow in Danny Bukantz's footsteps!

So I did something I thought I'd never do. I decided to stop fencing, at least for the current season. It was weird having so much free time, but it sort of felt right at the time.

Now, I was addicted to the sport. I was so addicted that I continued to compete at the national events, and, without training, still had some pretty good results. Actually, I enjoyed the competition more than ever before, probably because I was putting less pressure on myself. I always enjoyed the camaraderie of the fencing community, and I loved the boys' weekends around the country at these events.

As the spring of 1986 arrived, so did a decision that I would have to make. That decision was whether or not I would train for the upcoming US National Championships, which would be held at Manhattan College in Riverdale, New York that June.

Well, as it turned out, my season away from training totally energized me, and I regained the urge to compete at a high level. So I made the decision to practice at the Fencers Club once a week during the six weeks prior to the Nationals. It wasn't a lot, but it was just enough to sharpen up and get my competitive juices flowing again.

But I remained realistic. I knew that my last-minute, totally half-assed training schedule would be the equivalent of what I normally did in the first two weeks after Labor Day! I went into the 1986 Nationals to have fun and try not to completely embarrass myself or my dad, who would be in the stands rooting me on.

The men's foil championship was scheduled on Father's Day that year. That date meant plenty to me; my daughter Stephanie had been born in January, and this would be my first Father's Day as a father.

As was the norm, I qualified out of the preliminary pools and made it to the direct elimination. The DE round normally started at thirty-two, but on this day it started with the top sixteen, which was a break in my favor, as I was far from being in my best shape. However, the gym wasn't air conditioned, and the temperature was in the 90s. To make matters far worse, the humidity was near one hundred percent.

In short, the gym was the equivalent of hell for the fencers. We wear uniforms made of bulletproof Kevlar, and it is just an absolute sweatbox. I always sweat profusely; on that day, I actually sweated right through my uniform.

I only had to win two direct elimination bouts to reach the elite round of eight. The first bout was against my Fencers Club teammate Ted Pryor. Pryor was a tough and tricky fencer, but he had never beaten me in competition. And, while the bout stayed very close, I pulled off a 10-7 win.

The winner of my next bout would reach the finals. And I couldn't have drawn a better opponent. I would face Peter Burchard from California to get into the final eight. Burchard had achieved much higher results and rankings than Pryor, but I had had a winning streak against him since we first met in 1978! Wow! I was undefeated against him for seven years, which in fencing is totally unheard of.

Although Burchard would have been a tough draw for most, it didn't appear that way for me. Unfortunately, the winning streak ended on that hot, stuffy afternoon in Riverdale. Burchard nipped me 10-8. I was stunned and really annoyed at myself for having failed to capitalize on this golden draw. But, I still had a chance to make the finals. All I'd have to do was win one bout in the repecharge (loser's bracket).

I was dead tired, dehydrated, and felt like I had nothing left in the tank. Fortunately, I wasn't alone.

Incredibly, as if out of a nightmare, the opponent standing in my way to the National Championship finals would be a familiar face: Eric Rosenberg. We had fenced each other in a high school meet in 1972. We fenced each other at the previous summer's World Maccabiah Games in Israel. Now we would come full circle as we battled for a spot in the finals at the 1986 US National Championship.

Before the bout, Dad offered his usual reassuring advice, "Keep your distance and move your legs." It sounds simple and primitive, but as I've said time and again, it proved to be profound throughout my career.

Eric, as it turned out, was also dehydrated. He had cramped badly during his previous bout against my arch-nemesis Greg Massialas and was likely to do so again. Sure enough, he started cramping early on in our bout. Cramping or not, Eric was always a very dangerous fencer. And, as he knew my game inside and out, he was doubly dangerous for me.

He became even more dangerous while cramping! Like a wounded animal, his already unpredictable reactions became, if this was possible, even more unpredictable. Additionally, the cramps limited his ability to use his legs, so he remained on defense the entire bout.

This worked against me, because my strength, and the reason I usually beat Eric, was utilizing my defense against his attacks. So now he wouldn't be attacking; I had no choice but to go after him, which was a serious disadvantage for me, because attacking was not my forte, and Eric did have an excellent defense. To make matters worse, that defense would now be ultra-unpredictable; Eric was trying different tactics to adapt to his cramping.

As Eric wouldn't or couldn't attack, and I was extremely scared to, the bout had more feeling out than normal. We were both tentative and afraid to make mistakes. Quite frankly, I hated the thought of having to attack Eric when we practiced at the club, but, for crying out loud, this was to get into the National finals!

We went touch-for-touch until the score was 6-6. At that point, the time limit ran out, which meant whoever landed the next touch would win the bout and go onto the finals. It was sudden death and I didn't want to die – I especially didn't want to die to Eric, whether he was cramping or not.

Before the referee gave us the command to resume fencing, I decided that I would win or lose on a pre-planned action. I wouldn't allow myself to be surprised by a crazy action from the more-unpredictable-than-ever Rosenberg.

In those fleeting seconds, I thought about the logistics of the situation. Rosenberg probably wouldn't attack. He was almost sure to counterattack or parry my attack. Over the years, he had shown a propensity for counterattacking on the deciding touch of a bout. While this was a poor tactic, as it had a low percentage of landing a touch, it sometimes had the effect of surprising the opponent.

I decided that Rosenberg wouldn't just counterattack in this case, but because of his limited ability to move, he'd also duck down while executing the action. In order to hit him when he ducked, I would have no option but to hit him on his exposed back. In order to execute my action properly, I would have to make sure of three things: I'd have to push Rosenberg to his end of the fencing strip to minimize any surprise offensive actions, set up the attack from the proper distance, and make sure my first step was small and slow.

If the first step of my attack was either too big or too fast, I would be vulnerable to Rosenberg's eventual counterattack.

It was show time. I pushed Rosenberg toward the end of the strip, faking an attack the entire time so as to keep him on the defense. Then I saw my opening and knew it was then or never.

I took a slow and small first step, and then the rest happened in the blink of an eye. Sure enough, Rosenberg resorted to his usual move (while it surprised some, I was expecting it) of counterattacking. And, true to my prediction, he ducked down at the same time. On this one action, I had perfectly predicted my opponent's reaction.

But I still had to execute flawlessly. If I missed Rosenberg's back, his counterattack would score and he'd win the bout. After preparing the attack with my initial slow and small first step, I was in position to lunge and score the deciding touch. I saw his back open up, I lunged, and kaboom! I got him!

I did feel a little remorse for Rosenberg, as he'd never made a National final. But I got over it as I celebrated wildly and gave a great big hug to my Dad, who had been watching the bout from the side of the strip. Rosenberg, by the way, needed an hour and a half of intravenous fluids after the bout.

After having taken a break from training for almost the entire year, I accomplished what I used to train night and day for an entire year to do: I made the finals of the US National Fencing Championships.

At this point I was playing with the casino's money. Already I had done much better than expected. And, when I saw who my opponent would be in the round of the top eight, I was basically ready to cash in my remaining chips. The bout would be against Greg Massialas, who, along with Michael Marx, had dominated foil in the US for the last decade.

Not only would Massialas prove to be nearly impossible to beat under the best of circumstances, but my gas tank was nearly empty. And, to be quite candid, I hated him and he hated me. We were mortal enemies.

I didn't think I could win. In fact, I told Dad that I would instead try to clobber Massialas, as I knew that would give me some solace in losing. He was aware of my antipathy towards Massialas, but would have none of that unsportsmanlike talk. Dad sternly said, "Why don't you go out and beat him instead?"

Easier said than done, Dad.

Well, the stars must have been aligned on that Father's Day in 1986. Somehow, with Dad on the side cheering me on, I beat my nemesis 10-7. He expected to finish first or second that day, where he usually placed. Let's just say that we were equally stunned by the result.

As I came off the strip, still somewhat incredulous at the result, it didn't take two seconds before Dad said, "I told you the best way to get back at him was to beat him!"

I was on cloud nine and in the midst of a Magical Mystery Tour. The mindset of playing with the casino's money started morphing into the thought of trying to win the elusive National Championship. This was closer than I'd ever been – the top four!

No rest for the weary – the next bout would be against Marx. Marx was the best fencer of his era. He won eight US Nationals (Dad won four) and made five Olympic Teams (Dad made four).

But, while Marx was much better than me, I had above-average success against him. I was in the same situation as Rosenberg found himself in against me. Against Marx, I was the underdog.

If I went toe-to-toe with Marx, I'd be cooked. He was a physical specimen. At the end of a competition he was in better shape than I was at the beginning. He was fast; he was long; he was a machine. I had to keep good distance and try to slow the bout down from a footwork standpoint. As it was, my tongue was hanging out of my mask already. Sweat had long since permeated my Kevlar uniform.

The bleachers were packed with many New York friends cheering me on. The bout began.

I fenced according to plan and stayed away from the footwork follies that would tire me out and give Marx the advantage he didn't need. The bout went back and forth. I was holding my own. At one point, the sweat from my uniform actually shorted out the electric scoring machine, and the technicians took about half an hour to figure out what the problem was. They finally determined that I would have to change every bit of clothing, including my mask, as my excessive perspiration was causing the malfunction! With my somewhat sizeable physique it wasn't easy finding pants that fit, but teammate Jerome Demarque had a similarly-sized butt.

The breather certainly helped me, as I was feeling like a wilted flower.

The bout progressed to where my defense was getting the upper hand on the man with the best attack in the country. I was keeping the distance magnificently, which allowed me to parry Marx's attacks and score on the famous "counter-four riposte."

Dad's tactics were working in my favor against the best fencer of my time. And he was sitting right there, with a big smile on his face.

Incredibly, I hit on another counter-four riposte to make the score 9-7 in my favor. Oh, my God! I was one touch away from the gold medal bout. I never thought I'd get this close.

At 9-7, I knew Marx would expect me to go back to old faithful, the bear-trap counter-four parry. So, I pulled out a move I had waited the entire match to try. Instead of a fastball, I threw Marx a curveball in the way of a septieme (seventh) parry, which went in the opposite direction and would surprise Marx.

Okay – here we go. This final touch would get me to the big bout for the championship. Marx, like clockwork, attacked. I, like counter-clockwise, did the surprise parry. I caught his blade perfectly. Now, all I had to do was hit him on his open target, the right shoulder. I thrusted and went straight for Marx's shoulder.

Then I woke up. The dream had ended.

My point skipped off Marx's shoulder without registering. Not only did I miss the winning touch, Marx scored on his second action, a remise. Instead of the bout deservedly ending at 10-7, it was now 9-8.

Bad luck, bad timing, and bad vibes.

Marx scored the next three touches to win 11-9. I fenced as

well as I could and had nothing to be ashamed of. I sometimes took these close losses to top fencers as moral victories. But not this time. I'd had him, but I couldn't close the deal.

Although I was completely out of gas, I still had to regroup for the bronze medal bout. It would be against Dave Littell, another top guy. Littell, a former pro tennis player, was in tip-top shape, so I would have my work cut out for me – again.

I fought my hardest. I left nothing on the strip. But after a grueling half-hour bout, Littell prevailed 10-8.

(Massialas, Marx, and Littell would all make the 1988 Olympic Team, by the way.)

It was a brutally long day. I was totally gone, both physically and emotionally. And, same as the sad script from the 1981 World Maccabiah Games, I took fourth. Ugh.

I was so close to greatness on this day, but by its end, I was only fourth. It was hard to be disappointed, but after tasting a shot at a National Championship – Dad's National Championship – the great result had a hollow feel to it.

Oh well, on to the medal ceremony, where all of the eight finalists would receive one. And, I'm sure all of my teammates and friends would be there to give me a great, big cheer. That would put a nice exclamation point on the long and oppressively hot day at the Manhattan College gym.

But then something happened that made everything else that took place on this roller coaster ride of a competition pale in comparison. The person who received the honor of handing out the medals was United States fencing legend, and my dad, Danny Bukantz!

So when my name was called to come up and be recognized, Dad had the biggest grin on his face when he placed my hard-earned medal, the medal earned employing his tried-and-true tactics, around my sweaty neck. We hugged, everyone cheered, and my eyes welled up with tears.

In a competitive career that would span nearly twenty years, this was the one moment that topped all the others.

And there on that stage, on Father's Day, 1986, my first as a father, I was the luckiest man on earth to have my father, the man whom I revered and whose legacy I was chasing, present me with my National Championship medal.

That single moment made all the years of self-inflicted pressure completely worthwhile. Best of all, Dad and I got to share the moment.

It was a great Father's Day present for both of us... Sure beat getting a tie!

20

Jeff the Ref Returns

After winning the 1989 World Maccabiah Games gold medal in foil – Dad's gold medal – my competitive career was basically over. I just didn't have the drive to keep going for a spot on the 1992 Olympic Team after just missing it 1984 and 1988.

I stopped training entirely, but I continued to fly around the country to compete in national events. These weekends allowed me to stay in the sport, see my old friends, and compete, which was still my passion.

At this stage of my fencing career, my results in competitions were significantly less important; I was just having fun. Yes, fun! For the first time, with the pressure finally off, I was actually enjoying myself.

However – I was a lifer, after all – I still managed to do reasonably well in the competitions, so I kept competing through the end of the 1994 season. By this point, my days in the top ten, where I basically lived between 1981 and 1992, were over.

As it happened, in 1996 the Olympics were to be held in Atlanta, and the United States would be allowed to bring eight fencing referees as opposed to the maximum of one per country. I knew that I had to be one of the top eight referees in the country. Top eight? Ha! I was definitely one of the top three!

But there was a piece of unfinished business that I had to deal with before waltzing into the Atlanta Games as a fencing referee.

It had always bothered me that I never got my due as an international referee. Based on the poor treatment I had received between 1986 and 1988 from the FIE, my walking away was the right decision for me at that time.

But that decision left a void in my career. I was still considered the best, or one of the best refs in the country for foil, and I regularly received gold medal bout assignments at the Nationals, NACS, and NCAA tournaments. Those in charge of assigning me to these significant bouts – my peers – basically concurred. An anonymous survey of fencers commissioned by fencer Terrence Gargiulo reported similarly.

So, after getting the "okay" from my wife Carol, I decided to make the commitment necessary to get me to Atlanta. It would be a seamless transition, as I'd be replacing competition trips with refereeing trips during the 1995 and 1996 seasons.

If not for the possibility of Atlanta looming, I probably would have just continued competing.

My mind was made up about Atlanta. Carol and the rest of my family supported me. Being selected as one of the eight American referees would be a cinch. Finally, I would get the international recognition that I deserved.

Whoa! Not so fast, Jeff the Ref.

There were two gigantic obstacles to overcome in order to get the nod for Atlanta.

I really burned a lot of bridges in 1988 when I left the Junior Worlds a day early and thumbed my nose at Chaba

Pallaghy and Ralph Zimmerman. In addition, those in the
FIE have excellent long-term memories, and they do not take
kindly to any show of insubordination.

Well, the FIE was still around, of course. And, as it turned
out, Pallaghy had become a vice-president in the FIE and Chair
of the FIE's Referees Commission. Zimmerman had become
the Chair of the USFA's Referees Commission.

These two would either block or pave my way to the 1996
Olympic Games.

The reality was that they broke their promise to me back
in 1988. My response to that broken promise was appropriate,
regardless of insulting those higher up in the fencing pecking
order.

As Pallaghy was still a great family friend, and Zimmerman
didn't harbor a grudge, I decided to approach them directly,
albeit one-on-one.

I told them about my intentions and expectations for
Atlanta. They told me there was only one major problem: the
eight referees would have to come from the FIE's "approved"
list.

As I hadn't been officiating internationally, I was nowhere
to be found on that list.

"Well," I told them, "There is no way I'm not in the top
eight in the country. You tell me what I have to do to get onto
that 'approved' list and I'll do it."

Their solution to my new problem: I would have to start
traveling to Europe and referee at World Cups so I'd be back on
international radar. "But," they warned, "there is no guarantee
that you'll either make the 'approved' list or be one of the elite
eight selected for the Olympics."

I reiterated. "Tell me what I must do in the next two years.
I'll do my job, and I expect that you'll do yours."

By nature, I am not at all cocky. But, there are times
when you have to call a spade a spade. I had been, for over a
decade, the #1 foil ref in the United States. Getting onto that

FIE "approved" list wouldn't be a problem, as Pallaghy was the Chair of the Commission that made the list. Getting assigned by the US to go to World Cups would be up to Zimmerman.

I was very candid with them. I said that they owed me from the 1988 debacle in South Bend, and that they couldn't look me in the eye and tell me I'm not one of the top eight referees in the country. They couldn't.

Then I said, "Well, if you agree I'm one of the top eight, it's your job to get me selected for the 1996 Atlanta Olympic Games. No excuses."

My days of kissin' ass were over. I was a man of thirty-eight and a father of two. I was no longer the starry-eyed kid answering "Yes, sir" to anyone in the fencing hierarchy. I was frank, yet respectful. It was up to Pallaghy and Zimmerman to show me some respect, as well.

Before beginning work on this memoir, I called Pallaghy to clear something up. I asked him how he felt about my quitting in his face in 1988 and then coming back to him for help in 1994.

On my quitting, he said, "I was pissed, very upset. On a scale of one to ten, my anger at you was an *eleven*! You were already a great referee, and in a year or so would have been a major player internationally. I thought you made a big mistake, as I told you that day."

On my return, he exclaimed, "I was thrilled! After the long hiatus, you would have to start from scratch and climb all the way up the hill, but I knew you could do it. And, as always, I was right!"

During the 1995 season, I was sent to a few World Cups in Europe. I did well; I generally received assignments deep into the competitions. I started re-establishing my name. At the World Cup held in Atlanta, I refereed a bout in the top four with many FIE bigwigs watching.

And that was my long overdue break, so I made the best of it. Although I had many friends tell me I was perfect during the bout, leave it to the FIE brass to nitpick. Instead of complimenting me for doing a great job in a pressure-filled spot, they told me I looked a little nervous out there.

Can you believe these people? I just pitched a perfect game, and all they talk about is something totally irrelevant.

Actually, I took heed of that criticism, and subsequently tried very hard to look like the duck on top of the water. The reality is that the FIE prefers European refs who officiate with a disinterested look of disdain on their faces. Yep! That's the attitude they like. They like the cool cats.

Well, that's not my style. I'm interested and move up and down the strip with the fencers in order to keep the scoring machine and the fencers in my sightline at all times. I also make my calls with some enthusiasm. Screw the cool style of the Euro-refs!

For me, being cool is all about making the right calls. For me, being cool is all about making the fencers feel comfortable. For me, being cool is about substance, not style.

However, I resigned to try very hard to discipline myself while refereeing to look as relaxed as possible whenever I officiated in front of the FIE people. After all, they controlled my destiny for Atlanta.

After the 1995 season, I made it onto the FIE "approved" list. All that was left to do was make the top eight.

The 1996 season brought more World Cups and another successful performance during the finals of the pre-Olympic World Cup in Atlanta that spring. I believe that perfect game was met with the following FIE comment: "Well, your jacket wasn't buttoned, and you shouldn't chew gum when officiating in the finals."

You think I'm making this up?

FIE muckety-mucks speak perfect French, but the two words "bon" and "travail" are not part of their vocabulary. But, I didn't need their approval to know I did "good work."

With the decision for Atlanta coming up shortly after this competition, I was once again relegated to holding my breath. I still had very bad memories of holding my breath while waiting to hear my name called by the FIE in the past.

I promised myself I would never subject myself to the treatment I received at the Junior Worlds back in the late '80s, which is why I ended up quitting in the first place. Yet here I was again.

I walked away that time dejected, but with my head held high. However, failure to get selected for Atlanta would be a deathblow to my self-esteem and my enthusiasm. I continued to hold my breath.

During the first week of May, the FIE Referees Commission would hold a meeting in Paris to finalize the list of referees for the Games. Although I expected to get one of the eight American referee nods, there were eight other competent American refs. Someone would be the odd man out. Politics rule, and the FIE often operates in strange and mysterious ways.

On Sunday night I received a call from Zimmerman.

"Jeff," he said, "Chaba just called from Paris. You made it."

So, eight long years after telling the international refereeing community to stick it, they had selected me to represent the US as an Olympic referee.

Finally! I would see if I really was one of the best in the world.

Finally! I would have a chance to fill another of Dad's footsteps.

Finally! I would have a chance to make my own footsteps.

I flew to Atlanta with newfound confidence. In the last two years, I had officiated many times in Europe, done a few finals, and was a familiar (and now welcome) face to the fencers, coaches, and the FIE assignors.

As this trip was to be the culmination of two decades of hard work, I wanted to make sure that those closest to me would be there in Atlanta. I arranged for Carol to fly down for a few days. I asked my parents to come, but as they weren't fond of traveling anymore, Dad balked. That didn't fly with me, so I just purchased two tickets for them, booked a hotel, and told them I'd see them down there.

"Dad," I said incredulously, "do you think I've come this far for you to miss it?"

On Monday, July 22, 1996, my dream came true.

I was assigned to referee a bout in the top four of the men's individual foil event between Alessandro Puccini of Italy and Franck Boidin of France. The winner would proceed to the Olympic gold medal bout.

The pressure was enormous. I had had some major run-ins with the Italian team during the previous two years, including an incident in Havana when 1988 Olympic Champion Stefano Cerioni held a chair over my head and threatened to cold-cock me! That was a scene straight out of a professional wrestling match.

And the French were notorious for being rough on referees, to boot. In short, the Italians and the French were the worst to referee, as they complained about every call, and rode the referees consistently and mercilessly.

So, my work was cut out for me, which was just the way I liked it. I always felt I was as good as any foil referee in the world, and now I would finally have the golden opportunity to prove it.

It was either "put up" or "shut up."

My bout was slated to start around 4 p.m. The fencing venue at the Georgia World Congress Center was packed to its 4,000-seat capacity. The bout was going to be televised live throughout the world, which included the Eurosport broadcast, basically the ESPN of Europe.

As the pressure mounted, I was hooked up with a wireless microphone. Then, in one of those rare moments when I held my breath knowing my name *would* be called, the announcement came, "*Le arbitre pour le match, Monsieur Jeffrey Bukantz, Etas Unis.*"

I walked up to the three-tiered stage. The fencers were above me on the top tier; I was alone on the lowest tier; the 4,000 fencing fanatics were behind me. (Well, the fans were in back of me; I'm sure they were not all "behind" me!)

The omnipotent and omnipresent FIE brass were seated in the first row, only a few feet behind my khaki-clad butt. (Undoubtedly more concerned about my panty lines than my calls!)

In addition to the whole spectrum of pressure-invoking elements, I would, of course, have to speak French while I refereed, which always proved a bit daunting.

Oh, and one other aspect that posed potential problems: there would be two gigantic video screens, one on each side of the strip. After each touch, a red light would appear on the floor of the middle tier of the stage. This would signify a replay being shown on television, and that I had to wait until the light was off to recommence the bout.

I knew that if I watched those replays on the giant screens and saw that I blew a call, I could be blown away mentally for the rest of the bout. So, I forced myself to never look up, but rather stare at the red light until it went off.

Of course, if I blew a call, I wouldn't need to see the replay. The fans would let me hear about it. And, when it came to jeering and heckling, the French and the Italians were tied for first place.

This was the epitome of an "out-of-body experience," as the whole thing was so overwhelming. I joked with friends that I would probably need a change of underwear after the bout.

As the bout was set to begin, I thought back to my Bar Mitzvah, which took place twenty-six years earlier. Although I knew my *Haftorah* (the passage I had to read in Hebrew) cold, my knees were still shaking when I chanted. That physical reaction was something I had no control over, but I was internally calm because I was prepared.

And, I was likewise prepared for this moment. Oh, was I prepared.

I had prepared for this moment for over twenty years. Thousands and thousands of bouts: high school bouts. Collegiate bouts. National Championship bouts. World Cup bouts. Junior and Senior World Championship bouts. Practice bouts at the club. Unimportant early-round bouts. Crucial gold medal bouts. I had done it all, except an Olympic finals bout.

But this journey wouldn't have been worth the sacrifice if I didn't give my best performance during this Olympic final bout. Getting the assignment wouldn't be good enough.

I had to ace this test – the biggest one of my life. There would be no second chances or do-overs.

The next fifteen minutes would define my entire career. I had to turn that long-standing question mark about my international competency into a big, fat exclamation point.

The bout began with my command of "*Allez.*"

Puccini and Boidin traded touches as they battled to reach fifteen. Along the way, there were quite a few close calls. Once or twice, I heard some scattered catcalls from the stands. My Dad told me afterwards that one of those catcalls came from my friend, Frenchman Bruno Royer, who, not knowing he was sitting next to my dad, hollered, "Bukantz, go home!"

I felt eerily calm as the bout evolved. I knew I was in the zone – a special feeling referees get when they see the actions clearly and almost in slow-motion.

But, I knew all too well from experience that if I relaxed for one second or lost concentration, I could blow the call that could change the outcome of the bout. And, if that happened, it would change the outcome of my reputation forever.

I never once looked up at the video replay screens.

I made the calls without any hesitation.

I even threw in some nasal-sounding commands to sound extra French-like.

Puccini scored the fifteenth touch and won the bout. (He then went on to win the gold medal.)

Both fencers, as is the custom, shook my hand.

I knew I had aced the test. As I stepped off the raised platform, beaming with a feeling of pride I had never felt before, I was approached by one of the FIE guys. True to form, he didn't commend me or thank me for doing a superb job. Instead, without even shaking my hand, he said, "Jeff, your hand signals were not quite correct."

Need I say more?

But, I didn't need their accolades or approval. I knew right away how I performed. And you know what? I performed much better here than I did at my Bar Mitzvah. You know why? Because I practiced a hell of a lot harder for a hell of a lot longer. I couldn't wait for the Bar Mitzvah to be over; I didn't know if my Olympic moment would ever arrive.

The Bar Mitzvah, according to Jewish religion, is the rite of passage that transforms a boy into a man.

The Olympic final – the successful Olympic final – was the rite of passage that made me a man in the world of international fencing. As Pallaghy told me later that evening, "Bukantz, you are now considered to be one of the best referees in the world. Congratulations, my son."

It was the rite of passage that officially and finally enabled me to fill Danny Bukantz's footsteps.

It was the right of passage that enabled me to begin making footsteps of my own.

* * *

Postscript

Dad always said that being a referee guaranteed the following: "The fencers who love you will be like an ever-decreasing concentric circle. Eventually, everyone will remember the one call they think you blew in an important bout."

I refereed the Puccini-Boidin bout in July of 1996. The next time I saw Boidin was eight years later, at the 2004 Olympic Games in Athens. I went to introduce myself and see if he remembered me. Without a blink, he said, "Of course I remember you. You did a great job in Atlanta, but you made one mistake against me."

Post-postscript

I will always be Danny Bukantz's son. And, in the fencing world, I was always happy to be Danny Bukantz's son.

Yes, I wanted to make my own name. But, because I love Dad so much, and despite the pressure that came with being Danny Bukantz's son, I took great pride in my role.

I took great pride in being his son regardless of my success or failure in the sport.

From the day I was born, September 17, 1957, I had always been Danny Bukantz's son.

But, on July 22, 1996, the day I refereed the finals of the Olympic Games, something changed.

After my bout, I walked to the stands to sit with Carol, Mom, and Dad. They were so happy for me, and showering me with hugs, kisses, handshakes, and kudos. Everyone around them was as well, including some friends who flew to Atlanta from other parts of the country.

And, amazingly, two of those friends were Eric Rosenberg and Mitch Dorfman, the two guys who first humbled me in front of Dad at the Cardozo vs. Forest Hills high school meet nearly a quarter of a century earlier.

Also in this grouping, almost next to my dad, was Bruno Royer. Despite his public declaration for me to "go home," I had stayed.

I introduced Bruno to my parents and he laughed when he realized he had publicly berated their son only a few minutes earlier.

But, without knowing that my dad was even a fencer, let alone a legendary one, he surprisingly blurted out, "Oh, you're Jeff Bukantz's father!"

Dad told me that hearing Royer say that was his happiest and proudest moment, as he was so thrilled for me that on that day I was no longer just Danny Bukantz's son.

21

Fly the Flag

I've always been patriotic. But, as with many Americans, my patriotism used to be an internal burning, not necessarily an outwardly loud and proud kind. After all, how could anyone not appreciate our country, the greatest and most giving country in the world?

And how could I not be? I was the son of a World War II veteran and a Holocaust survivor. To not understand the importance of full-fledged patriotism would have been a crime. I always did, so no problem there. I will always love my country, despite the many people in the United States who never will.

Those who don't respect the brilliance of America feel guilty about its greatness and resent some of the most important aspects of the country. There are even "Americans" who resent our successes in the Olympics, and, as it goes hand in hand, even despise the nationalistic chant of "USA! USA!" In their warped minds, it's not cool to wear USA outfits or root for their team. And I think, because of their ever-present negative attitudes, even real patriots succumb to the peer pressure.

I know that I sometimes held off from beginning USA chants; the negative attitudes have communicated the air of "The Ugly American" whenever these chants begin in a world competition.

I spent my entire fencing career trying to follow in Dad's footsteps. I wanted to win a national championship. I wanted to make the Olympic Team. And, yes, I wanted to qualify for an international team and receive the vaunted USA sweatsuit and then proceed to parade around in it, advertising my greatness and my love of country.

And I wanted that sweatsuit to be as bold and as loud as possible. RED, WHITE, and BLUE! Stripes, stars, a big USA patch… you name it. I wanted the USA chant to explode out of the fabric.

And then, in 1981, I finally earned my first sets of USA sweats when I made both the Maccabiah Games and the World University Games. Yes, 1981 was a great year as I received two sets of US sweats to begin my collection.

And then, after picking up my beloved new wardrobe, the sweats went back into my closet, never to be worn again.

You're probably wondering, "Wait a second, Mr. USA! Where's your patriotic pride now?"

Well, there was a method to my madness. I felt that by wearing these USA sweats at competitions my opponents would have had even more incentive to beat me. Can you believe that? I worked so hard to get something, and then after reaching the mountaintop, I completely refused to parade around in the sweats I was so proud to have earned.

Along the way, I've made plenty of teams and received many different USA sweat suits. In 1993, I received the loudest and proudest sweats ever from the US Maccabiah Team. The jacket was basically a red, white, and blue flag. It was beautiful, and, for me, it epitomized exactly what a USA sweatsuit should look like. Yet I wouldn't wear it because of the aforementioned reason.

And yes, it hung in my fencing closet, never worn, from the summer of 1993 until September 12, 2001.

You see, my whole attitude changed after September 11.

We all remember where we were, who we were talking to, what channel we were watching when the disaster struck. We all know how it affected us. We all know the sadness and the hatred we felt. We all know we were basically numb from disbelief.

For me, I just remember thinking how proud I was to be an American. And I knew, from that tragic moment on, that I would never again shrink away from showing that love of country, especially when it came to wearing the red, white, and blue USA sweats.

Starting the very next day, I wore the 1993 ultra-loud Maccabiah set. I wore it to my son Michael's baseball games. I wore it to the New York Rangers pre-season hockey game at Madison Square Garden, the very first sporting event held in the city after the attacks. There were television crews all over the place in front of the Garden. And every one of them came over to interview the man who would become known that night as the "Flag Man."

After September 11, the sweats that I had always deemed too loud to wear in public became, in my mind, the coolest outfit I could possibly put together. It was no longer about personal pride in having earned them or in showing them off, but rather about an unmitigated and unchecked patriotism.

I didn't give a crap about how the anti-America crowd felt. "Screw them!" I thought. I was proud as hell to be an American, and I wanted everyone to know it. And, if anyone had a problem with my patriotism, I was ready to take 'em on.

Fighting words? Maybe. But there comes a time when you fight for what you believe in, and I wasn't going to be deterred by the "Hate America First" crowd. Some of those nitwits went so far as to claim that we deserved September 11, as if we're the bad guys in the world. All the more reason to make them squirm when I wore the sweats or started up a rousing USA chant. What are these people thinking? If they're so upset with their country, why don't they just leave?

Whenever I think of such imbeciles, or have to defend the United States in their twisted minds, I paraphrase what Tony Blair said about alleged anti-American sentiment in the world: "You can determine the popularity of a country by looking at how many people want to get in and how many want to get out."

How profound. What a way to stop the naysayers cold in their tracks. What a way to erase any or all doubts about our country. As I said, let the losers leave if they want to. But, they always seem to stay, hmm....

At the end of the day, the irony is that *they* are the Ugly Americans they purport to despise so much!

Anyway, while my patriotism only grew after September 11, little did I know what the fencing road would bring, as I was retired from competing but still refereeing. However, a new and exciting chapter in my fencing career was about to begin.

* * *

In 2003, I was named Team Captain for both the Junior and Senior World Championship Teams. In addition, I was named to the Pan American Team. Lots of sweats, lots of pride, lots of unfettered displays of patriotism at these events in Sicily, Cuba, and the Dominican Republic.

And I'll be damned if any of the naysayers deterred me from my love of country, wearing my USA sweats or chanting "USA! USA!" whenever our teams needed a boost.

On December 26, 2003, a thirty-two-year goal would finally be reached. On a conference call of the USFA's High Performance Committee, I was named the Team Captain for the 2004 Olympic Fencing Team. Thirty-six years after experiencing my first Olympic Games in Mexico City, and after being a part of the games as a referee, I was finally going as part of the United States *Team!*

Of course, my original goal was to be a competitor in the Olympic Games, but I had become a member of the prestigious team and that was good enough for me.

It really was a dream come true. And, to boot, my folks were able to share this important moment with me – the culmination of a son's lifelong pursuit to follow in his dad's footsteps!

Personal pride aside, I was just so proud to represent my country. You already know about my patriotism, but after September 11, I was never keeping those feelings to myself again. I couldn't wait to march into the Olympic Stadium in Athens wearing the loudest red, white, and blue sweats possible and wave to the crowd as they chanted "USA! USA!"

In Athens, I would fulfill a family legacy and the lifelong dream of representing the United States at the single event that most epitomized national pride.

However, on May 17, 2004, only weeks before I was to board a plane to Athens, I was literally and figuratively in for a rude awakening.

On May 16, newspapers all over the world reported that Mike Moran, a consultant for the United States Olympic Committee (USOC), suggested that US Olympians should "cool it," as *The London Sunday Telegraph* put it.

Okay, fair enough. No Olympian should taunt an opponent under any circumstances. No one competing at the Games should be doing Hulk Hogan-like poses with his or her country's flag. (Like the US 4x100 relay team did during the 2000 Summer Olympics in Sydney.)

But Moran, in fact, was also telling the athletes, "Don't run over and grab a flag and take it around the track with you."

I received this unsettling news on the morning of May 17th when a Boston radio show "Blute and Scotto" of WRKO phoned my house at 6:30 a.m. looking for the "Flag Man" to make a comment on Moran's remarks. My immediate response was, "How dare he?"

There is no comparison whatsoever between taunting and celebrating. For anyone to suggest that US athletes shouldn't celebrate a gold medal by taking a lap with the American flag in order to please someone else – for any reason – is downright incomprehensible and reprehensible.

Right is right; wrong is wrong. We all have to make our choices based on what we believe to be right or wrong, not based on what someone else thinks! And my opinion, as I presented it to the radio show hosts, is that it is perfectly acceptable to take a victory lap with the flag. We are representing our country at the Olympic Games – the event, as I've stated previously, that epitomizes what national pride is all about.

The bottom line is that the same people who despise us now will not despise us any less because we refrained from taking our flag around the venue in celebration. The thought is purely ridiculous and irrelevant. If we marched into the Opening Ceremonies and threw one hundred dollar bills into the crowd, there would still be those that hate us. "Who cares?" I wondered.

We have to compete with dignity and honor. While displays of bad behavior and taunting should be "cooled" at all costs, it's imperative that United States Olympians celebrate their victories in the manner that any other country would, and that definitely includes the proud display of the Stars and Stripes!

Shame on anyone to suggest otherwise, especially someone retained by the organization responsible for sending us!

Furthermore, why should we change our way of life based on someone else's beliefs? That's akin to giving in to those you abhor because you have a freedom they don't.

I told Blute and Scotto that I expected our athletes to do the right thing, not the politically correct thing. We're all proud to be Americans and we're going to show it. The beauty of living in this great country is that we have the right to celebrate no matter who tells us otherwise, and I have the right to vehemently disagree with the USOC's public behavior consultant.

Moran also informed the athletes that waving the American flag may be viewed as confrontational by others.

In another moment of disgust, I told the radio show hosts exactly what I would do in Athens. My mother once brought me a flag to display on Memorial Day and the Fourth of July. That morning I proclaimed, "My mom's flag will be the first item I pack for Athens, and if we win a medal, it damn well will go on a victory lap."

Well, on the surface, though I was being completely genuine, that comment was a little unintentional false bravado. The United States hadn't won an Olympic fencing medal since 1984 when Peter Westbrook won the bronze in men's saber.

Exactly three months later, on August 17th, Mariel Zagunis of Portland, Oregon, was in the women's saber gold medal bout. I was sitting with the team cheering wildly up in the stands. When Mariel scored the 10th touch of the 15-touch bout, I ran down to the floor to make sure the team would be able to run onto the strip to celebrate.

I was summarily stopped by a Greek female security guard, who said, "Sorry, but you can't go onto the floor."

"Wait a minute," I pleaded. "I'm the Captain of the American team and our fencer is about to win the gold medal!"

The petite young lady was not phased. "I'm sorry, sir, but I can't let you pass."

"Look," I said, "In about a minute, I'm leading the American team onto the floor to celebrate, and you have to let us go."

"Sorry sir, but you can't," she reiterated.

Uh, oh. This was serious. If we couldn't get onto the floor if Mariel won, the once-in-a-lifetime moment would be without the fencing tradition of tossing your champion three times into the air. It wouldn't ruin the moment – nothing could – but it would be void of the wonderfully exuberant celebration that occurs at the moment of a World or Olympic championship win.

This was just like a fencing bout, as I had to adjust and change tactics, and quickly. It was time to go to Plan B.

I told the security guard, in Greek, that she was beautiful, and handed her an American team pin.

She smiled, blushed a little, and then just said, "Okay, you can bring the team on."

That is exactly how it transpired. If you want to know why I knew the Greek word for beautiful, it'll be in my next book.

I sprinted back up to the stands to get the team ready. At the same time I was literally patting myself on the back, proud of my success with the guard and thinking I was the best Captain in the history of sports.

Mariel scored the 13th touch.

I jumped up from my seat, barked, "Let's go!" to the team, and we sprinted right back down to the entrance to the field of play. Super Captain had taken care of the rest.

We were so excited. This would be the first American Olympic gold medal in fencing in one hundred years.

As we zoomed around the corner of the bleachers towards the floor, I was in for a big surprise: The adorable little young lady guard was gone, and her replacement was a big, burly, mustachioed bruiser.

Oh, no! If I stayed with Plan B, which was to tell him in Greek that he was beautiful, he could only take it two ways… and neither was good for me!

So, on to Plan C!

There was no time for negotiation. What I wanted to say to him was, "Look, pal, we can do this the hard way or the easy way, but we're going onto the floor whether you like it or not!"

But he had a gun. I spotted the FIE's communications guru, Jochen Farber, and he knew that it was in the best interests of fencing to have this rare American celebration. Farber told the guard to let us on.

Not five seconds after, Mariel scored the Olympic gold medal touch. Imagine that: The United States waited for a century to win an Olympic fencing gold medal, and we came within five seconds of missing the fun.

The team stormed onto the floor and jumped up onto the raised strip. As if out of a bad dream, when we hit the strip, Mariel jumped off to go shake the referee's hand! Then the referee, worried that the FIE brass would blackball him, told the new Olympic Champion to salute her opponent. So much for spontaneity.

And the FIE wonders how fencing could get better television ratings?

Mariel excitedly jumped back up onto the raised strip, knowing that it was time for the celebration to finally begin.

At this moment, I could only think of one thing: I was Alice Bukantz's son.

Yes, I was the son of a wonderful person who would just be a Holocaust statistic, not *survivor*, if not for the United States saving her (and millions of others) in World War II. I wouldn't even be anyone's son if not for the greatest country in the world making that sacrifice. And, leave it to an immigrant to fully understand and appreciate why we are the greatest country. The Land of the Free, and the Home of the Brave!

Leave it to an immigrant, let alone a Holocaust survivor, to give her previously flag-less son a flag to display proudly on Memorial Day and the Fourth of July.

Before the team could take part in fencing's oldest tradition, I had to take care of business. When WRKO's Blute and Scotto woke me up on May 17th informing me of Mike Moran's incomprehensibly offensive comments suggesting that American athletes should not celebrate with the flag at the Games, I made a promise.

I made that promise from the heart, not thinking that I would ever be in the position to fulfill it.

I handed Mariel, whose infectious smile was already ear-to-ear, my mother's flag. Then, as per the custom, the team threw her into the air three times. Both Mariel and Old Glory were flying proudly for those precious seconds that will be forever frozen in time.

Mariel then took that Grand Old Flag on a victory lap, and that photo graced thousands of newspapers around the world. In that instant, she was beautiful, the moment was beautiful, and, best of all, the American flag was beautiful.

22

Rabbit Ears

Growing up as a member of the worldwide fencing community, any mention of my dad always elicited a happy smile, some amusing anecdote, and a heart-felt compliment. With effortless ingenuousness, he made friends with even his fiercest rivals. I never saw him behave discourteously or disrespectfully to anyone, or judge someone by his or her success on the fencing strip. Although an indomitable competitor, he is nonetheless a gentle soul who eschewed the heated confrontational approach in favor of calm, reasoned consensus. He had impressive credentials, but he always remained modest and self-effacing. Even as a dentist, he was gentle.

I may be prejudiced, but Dad deserves every honor and accolade he's ever received and then some.

While he has been elected into numerous Halls of Fame, he will forever be proudest of being an inaugural inductee into the City College of New York (CCNY) Alumni Varsity Sports Hall of Fame.

Danny Bukantz graduated from CCNY in 1938. He was the school's first-ever intercollegiate fencing champion, winning the individual foil event as a senior.

Dad was involved with the CCNY fencing program for the next twenty-five years: as an advisor, a recruiter, and a mentor to subsequent generations of students. He was City College's unofficial ambassador – the guy the administration went to for advice when hiring a coach or anything involving the fencing program.

In 1967, the CCNY Sports Hall was created. While the average person might roll their eyes and ask, "What's the big deal?" the fact is that CCNY was loaded with great athletes during my father's era. Henry Wittenberg was a 1948 Olympic gold medalist in wrestling; Nat Holman, also known as "Mr. Basketball," was one of the greatest coaches and players of all time. Both eventually would be elected into the International Jewish Sports Hall of Fame. Of course, there were plenty of other stellar athletes throughout the school.

In fencing, CCNY was loaded with Olympians such as Abe Cohen, Nat Lubell, Hal Goldsmith, and 1960 Olympic bronze medalist Albert Axelrod.

For the Hall's inaugural class, only one fencer was to be elected. Basically, it came down to Dad or Axelrod.

While Axelrod's Olympic medal spoke volumes for him, the committee of twenty-one unanimously elected Danny Bukantz.

My father was thrilled. Even though I was only nine at the time, I remember how much this meant to him. He loved his alma mater and devoted much of his adult life to giving back to the school, so he couldn't wait for the January 1967 induction dinner. All of his fellow alumni were very happy for him.

All but one.

One night at the Fencers Club, Axelrod approached my father and without warning or segue, said, "Danny, you should step down and allow me to go in the Hall in its inaugural year."

Caught off guard, Dad was incredulous. Uncharacteristically, he was beside himself. As a passionate defender of my father's legacy, I would have cold-cocked Axelrod or told him to screw himself. Dad, after regaining his bearings, simply looked at him and replied, "Albie, the committee selected me, and I have earned my right to receive that award."

It is truly amazing that under those circumstances Dad was able to answer in such a classy manner.

And then he walked away.

An athlete's level of success is typically determined by the amount of hardware he or she earned. The teams made, the championships won, the press clippings received...

But what makes a person great isn't the hardware. On the contrary, it's about the *software*. It's about having integrity and earning the respect and confidence of your peers. Axelrod had the hardware, the bronze medal. He defined himself by that piece of bronze. As a person, however, he was defined by his flawed software. While my father always went out of his way to be courteous and supportive, Axelrod always seemed to deliberately antagonize and be unnecessarily confrontational. Axelrod was as quick to humiliate a fellow fencer who disagreed with him as my father was to drop an unsolicited compliment.

Dad had a heart of gold, and Axelrod had a medal of bronze. That pretty much says it all.

The CCNY Sports Hall of Fame plaque has the following motto: "Character... Sportsmanship... Service."

It's no wonder that the twenty-one members voted unanimously for Dr. Daniel Bukantz.

I'll always remember that cold Tuesday night that January. I've never been prouder of my dad, and I've never seen him happier.

Axelrod and Dad were the top two foil fencers from their era. Both made four Olympic Teams. Axelrod won five individual titles and Dad four. They were always ranked #1 or

#2, and they completely dominated their event.

Until this unseemly move by Axelrod, they really didn't have any issues. In fact, they'd been roommates at a couple of Olympic Games. But after this, Axelrod took great pleasure in taking verbal shots at my dad. He would never do it to his face, but frequently within earshot of me. He was trying to get under my skin, and he did a very good job.

You see, I had big rabbit ears when it came to my dad. If anyone said anything bad about him as a person, fencer, or referee, they had to answer to me.

One night at the Fencers Club, Axelrod crossed the line. Very publicly, and with only a few feet separating us, he made some incredibly derogatory comment about my dad, who wasn't there to defend himself. Seeing red, I confronted this bully. In a split second, I dropped my foil and mask, and lurched at a surprised Axelrod. With my right hand, I grabbed him by the front of his T-shirt, cocked my left hand, and growled, "Listen, if I ever hear you say a bad word about my father again, I will break your nose. Do you understand?!"

Stammering, he sheepishly said, "All right."

Axelrod never uttered a mean word about my dad in front of me again. But his petty diatribes continued.

My dad's best friend was Alex Solomon. Alex was a decent fencer who once won the Midwest Saber Championship. When Alex's first wife passed away, he ate dinner at our home every night, and they lunched together near my dad's office for many years. They were true-blue friends. Alex, a longtime member and the official historian of the Fencers Club, took special pride in decorating the club with individual and Olympic Team photos of the FC legends. This became his passion. Alex always pointed out to me what he had put on Dad's photo, "*Olympian Extraordinaire,*" which was reflective not only of his competitive achievements, but his career as an Olympic referee.

When Alex passed away, he left a substantial endowment to the FC. Some of this money was earmarked to refurbish the extensive photographic archive he compiled on behalf of the club. There was a committee formed to handle the project. Axelrod volunteered to have the photographs matted and reframed and have the calligraphy redone.

One day, I received a call from my friend Eric Rosenberg, who was then President of the FC. He said, "Jeff, stay calm, but he's done it again."

"Who's done it again, Eric?" I asked.

"Albie," Eric replied.

"Well, what the hell has he done this time?"

Eric laid it on me, "Well, you know how Alex Solomon left money to the club to have the artwork redone? Well, they were redone. Only one thing missing. Albie had the words *'Olympian Extraordinaire'* removed from your dad's."

"Give me his home number, Eric."

"Jeff, let it go," he begged

"Eric, those two words mean nothing to my dad," I replied. "They meant something to Alex Solomon. Alex was my dad's best friend. And, that man had no right to do such a petty, hurtful thing."

My heart was pounding. I hated this man. I had to get it off of my chest. So, I called him.

He answered the phone and I tore into him. "Why would you do such a petty thing? Why would you hurt my father? Are you such a small man that this is what you have to resort to?"

Incredibly, Axelrod wouldn't own up to his chicanery, but said, "The committee decided. The committee decided that the word 'extraordinaire' was inappropriate."

I riposted, "By definition, his representing the United States at nine Olympic Games makes him an *extraordinary* Olympian." And, finally, I really let loose, "Listen, you lowlife, either you get it fixed or I'm going to rip it off the wall and do it myself!" I hung up with a pointed BOOM!

One week later, Axelrod had the calligrapher add the words *"Olympian Extraordinaire."*

Every old-timer in the fencing world has their Axelrod stories.

In 2001, the FC scheduled a novelty event called, "The Battle of the Ages." A match was arranged between some of the up-and-coming youth fencers (thirteen years old and younger) and the Club septuagenarians. Before the event, Rosenberg called me up and asked me to volunteer as a referee for the event.

Of course, I would. It was to be a fun evening, and I really wanted to see what the new crop of kids could do against guys that I grew up fencing against at the club. Heck, some of them were contemporaries of my dad!

I walked into the FC, now re-located at 25th Street and 7th Avenue, with a big smile on my face. While I take refereeing very seriously and strive for perfection every time, this was a night where there'd be no pressure on me at all.

Or so I thought.

In the third bout of the team event, Axelrod was matched up with a little tyke named Rebecca Hirschfeld. Even as an octogenarian, Axelrod was built like an ox. He was raw-boned, still muscular, devoid of fat, around six feet tall, and probably about two hundred-pounds. And, he was an Olympic medalist, to boot.

Rebecca was ten years old and probably weighed seventy pounds soaking wet.

After the first couple of actions, Axelrod complained to me that the little girl was turning her back, an illegal action warranting a yellow penalty card. I disagreed and told him to get back to his en garde line.

On the very next action, he took off his mask and started yelling at me "She's turning her back!"

At this point, I must admit my heart was pounding as I quickly tried to think of how best to handle his tantrum. The whole moment was so surreal, and I knew everyone watching, aware of my antipathy towards Axelrod, was waiting for me to explode.

Somehow, I kept my cool.

On the very next action, when the fencers got too close to each other, I called, "Halt!" loud and clear.

Axelrod, after the halt, pulled his fencing arm back and thrust it with maximum force into Rebecca's back. Rebecca was nearly in tears when I walked up to her and asked, "Young lady, how old are you?"

"I'm ten years old," she replied.

As I walked up to Axelrod, the tension in the FC rose in anticipation as to how I would respond. But instead of a punch in the nose, I quietly said to Axelrod, "That girl is ten years old. This is a friendly exhibition. Is there something seriously wrong with you?"

I figured that forcing him to confront his behavior would accomplish more than a punch. And it crossed my mind in those few seconds that this would have been how Dad might have handled it.

Though I've tried, I'm not exactly like Dad, so I needed something a little closer to the punch in the nose.

I asked Rebecca if she was okay, and then walked over to the team of youngsters. Very calmly, but loud enough for all the spectators and Axelrod to hear, I commented, "Did you guys see what just happened? Well, this was a learning experience for you. This is an example of how *not* to act when you grow up, okay?"

Axelrod eventually won the bout. After all he had accomplished in his life – an Olympic medal, National Championships – it was still extremely important for him to beat that ten-year-old girl. But, yet again, he lost face. It was ironic that a man so obsessed with getting the respect and accolades he felt he deserved never understood why others, like my dad, were treated with so much more regard.

In 2004, Albert Axelrod passed away. To the bitter end, he remained obsessed with his own legacy and frustrated over the fact that, like Rodney Dangerfield, he never got any respect. In my mind, Axelrod will always be the counterpoint to my father, the "ying" to his "yang." His obsessive need to prove himself, even after all he had accomplished as an athlete, drove him to alienate the very individuals from whom he sought approval. In some strange way, he helped me put into focus the positive qualities of my dad, that the software means more than the hardware, and I should be grateful for that.

Thanks, Albie… I guess.

23

The International Jewish Sports Hall of Fame

If you ever saw Joseph Siegman's book *Jewish Sports Legends*, you'd be shocked. The 302-page book is loaded with stories about Jewish Olympic medalists and about each member of the International Jewish Sports Hall of Fame (IJSHOF), which is located at the Wingate Sports Institute in Netanya, Israel.

By the way, there are still plenty of Olympic medalists who have not yet been elected into the IJSHOF, which only further illustrates how Jewish athletes have excelled.

In 1993 I was to compete in Israel at my fourth World Maccabiah Games, albeit only in the team events and acting as Team Captain. At the quadrennial event, the IJSHOF planned to hold its induction ceremony for those who'd been elected into the hall during the previous four years. Axelrod, thanks to his bronze medal at the 1960 Olympics in Rome, was to be inducted during the 1993 ceremony. When he couldn't make the trip, he asked me to accept his award and bring it back to the States. How's that for irony?

After attending the ceremony for Axelrod, I decided
to make an effort to get Dad into the IJSHOF. So when I
returned from Israel I went to work. Unfortunately, I was
immediately rebuffed by those I contacted. "We still have
Jewish fencers from Europe who won Olympic gold medals
who aren't in yet," I was told. "How Axelrod got in with just
a bronze was a surprise to the committee. It will be tough for
your dad despite his incredible credentials."

Phooey! But then I found out that the IJSHOF had
a category called The Pillar of Achievement. This was for
athletes, coaches, referees, administrators, media persons, team
owners, and any other related person who has done something
extraordinary in his or her sport.

Well, winning thirteen US National Championships and
representing the US at nine consecutive Olympic Games was
as extraordinary as it gets. So without an Olympic medal, it
was on to Plan B. But as it turned out, getting my dad into The
Pillar of Achievement was just as difficult.

No matter how many times I contacted the committee
or resubmitted his nomination and bio, it just didn't happen.
Then the years started to pass quickly; Danny Bukantz was
bypassed throughout the rest of the '90s.

I had pretty much given up hope and resigned myself that
while Dad would always be an inaugural member of the CCNY
Hall (1967) and the US Fencing Association Hall (1978), there
was nothing more I could do for him and the IJSHOF.

And then, in 2000, out of nowhere, I received a call from
Alan Sherman, President of the IJSHOF. "Jeff," he said, "I have
great news. We just voted your father into the Hall of Fame,
and I wanted you to be the first to know. Congratulations."

Okay, I admit it, I broke down and cried. And, as I type
this, my eyes are welling up again. It took seven years and a lot
of *chutzpah*. I never expected the day to come.

Believe me, the next phone call was the most wonderful
call I've ever made. I think I cried again and got so choked up

that I could barely get the words out. I know Mom and Dad were thrilled. It was weird, though, because I felt like Dad was more touched by my efforts on his behalf than actually getting into the Hall.

Sure enough, when I recently asked him how he felt when I told him the great news, he replied, "I was very, very flattered. But I was really proud of you for the effort you made."

The induction ceremony took place the following year at the 2001 World Maccabiah Games. While it was a great honor, Dad wasn't up for making the long trip to Israel. So was there ever any doubt about who *was* up for it?

Although the Intifada had reared its ugly head again and suicide bombs were exploding, I had no choice but to go. My family was dead set against it. To this day, my son Michael gets mad at me whenever the topic comes up. I tried to explain how important the journey would be for me, but to no avail. Quite frankly, even Dad suggested that I stay home. Well, he's forgiven; after all, he could never have known how much his election meant to me.

Anyway, I was off to Israel for something far more important than a competition. In fact, I planned to arrive the afternoon before the ceremony, attend it the next day at 11 a.m., and fly back to the States that night.

I spent quite a bit of time crafting the speech I was to give at the induction ceremony. I knew that it had to be short and with a message that best described why Danny Bukantz was worthy of their Hall of Fame.

It was brutally hot in Israel on the morning of the ceremony, so I decided it would be perfectly appropriate to wear dress shorts to the ceremony. Naturally, and this was guaranteed, I was the only person among the inductees to do so.

Oh, the humanity. I really wished Mom and Dad were able to attend, but come to think about it, I'm glad Mom wasn't there to dress me down! At least I shaved.

It was certainly a right of passage for me when I stood up to speak about my Dad. At that moment, I really didn't care if I made an impact with the people in the packed auditorium. All I could think about was how deserving my father was to be included in the International Jewish Sports Hall of Fame, how happy I was for him, how proud I was of him, and how incredibly lucky I was to be able to be representing him.

As I breezed through the tangible accomplishments, such as the thirteen US National Championships (four individual and nine team titles), the nine consecutive Olympic Games, and the various other Halls of Fame, I realized that it was the intangibles that really made Dad a Hall of Famer.

He didn't just win bouts on the fencing strip. He wasn't just a great referee. Rather, he was known throughout the United States and the world as man of unequalled integrity and honesty. Dad was known as someone who went out of his way to never embarrass another person, no matter the transgression. And, despite his world-class credentials as a fencer and a referee, Dad never talked about himself. He exuded class and modesty at all times.

Ultimately, Dad won the hearts of everyone within the fencing world.

It doesn't really matter that I said all those things on that boiling hot July morning in Israel. It doesn't matter that nobody in that room remembered a word of my speech anyway.

What matters is that everything I said was true.

And trust me, Dad; no one is prouder to have given your induction speech than me.

*   *   *

The day and a half in Israel was a whirlwind and, incredibly, after spending the afternoon with my cousin Yossi Makai, it was right back on the plane.

When the plane took off and I saw the lights fading behind me as we ascended over the Mediterranean, my mind was racing. Initially, I was relieved to have been safely out of range of any Palestinian homicide bombers. Then all I could think about was how cool this entire adventure had been, from submitting Dad's nomination back in 1993 until the long-awaited, albeit highly unexpected, election in 2000. And now, sweetest of all, was giving the induction speech in 2001.

It was such a satisfying moment, one that I didn't want to pass.

Inevitably, during the eleven-hour flight, I wondered what it would be like to be elected into a Sports Hall of Fame. My credentials weren't in the same league as Dad's… not many people's were.

But I'd had a pretty impressive resumé as a fencer and a referee as well. I dreamed that maybe someday I'd be fortunate enough to be elected into a Hall of Fame.

I dreamed that maybe someday I'd be lucky enough to share my special night with Mom and Dad.

And then, I dreamed that maybe someday if this all came true, Dad would be there to introduce me at *my* induction ceremony.

Before I knew it, I woke up as we landed at Newark. It was a rude awakening; I left one of those dreams you wish you could dive right back into.

No such luck. What happened in Israel was a dream come true for me. What I dreamt on the plane was, well, just a dream.

24

Winning Isn't Everything

Danny Bukantz left some King Kong-sized footsteps for his son to fill. But he never asked me to fill them; that I decided on my own.

My journey was a labor of love. And while I didn't particularly love the sacrifice and failure along the way, I do love fencing and I do love my dad.

In the three and a half decades since the fencing bug took full control over me at the 1972 Munich Olympics, I embarked on this journey that was guaranteed to fail.

You see, there was no way I thought I could do everything that Dad did, let alone *anything* that he did. He left me with two gigantic footsteps that were full of gigantic challenges:

1) Make an Olympic Team
2) Make Four Olympic Teams
3) Win the Individual US National Championship (let alone four!)

4) Win the US National Team Championship (let alone nine!)
5) Become an Olympic Referee
6) Officiate in the Olympic Finals
7) Win the gold medal in foil at the World Maccabiah Games
8) Make the International Jewish Sports Hall of Fame (let alone *any* sports hall of fame)
9) Qualify for a World Championship Team (let alone any international team)

These were all tangible accomplishments, and there could be no subjective, feel-good half measures for having giving it the old college try. Either I did, or I didn't.

So, at the end of the day, just how did I fare in my pursuit?

Well, to be honest, much better than I ever expected. Here's the rundown:

1) I made an Olympic Team, albeit as Team Captain
2) I won the US National Team Championship eight times
3) I became an Olympic Referee
4) I officiated the Olympic Finals
5) I won the gold medal in foil at the World Maccabiah Games
6) I made the New Jersey Jewish Sports Hall of Fame in its inaugural year
7) I qualified for three World Championship Teams: the World University Games Team, the Pan American Games Team, and three World Maccabiah Games Teams

Wow! Until I actually put this down on paper, I hadn't realized how many of my dad's accomplishments I had achieved for myself. Based on this list, there is no doubt that my difficult journey was worth every bit of effort. But would it have been worth it if I had not attained even one of my lofty goals?

Let's not kid ourselves. I had tunnel vision throughout the grueling three-and-a-half-decade journey. I always had specific, tangible goals and reaching them was the only thing I thought about. To claim otherwise would be less than candid.

While I was immersed in my life's journey, I focused primarily on the destination: attaining my dad's legacy. Now, looking back, I realize that I had it all wrong.

I defined myself by winning or losing, not by the fact that I had given everything I had.

To have a healthy life, one must learn to enjoy and appreciate the journey, regardless of whether or not you reach your desired destination. Otherwise, life would be chock-full of self-inflicted disappointments. If you don't enjoy and appreciate the effort, anything less than the ultimate prize at the finish line will leave you empty.

That's just not healthy. The late Green Bay Packers Coach Vince Lombardi was famous for saying, *"Winning isn't everything, it's the only thing."*

I firmly disagree with the renowned Hall of Fame Coach. Everyone strives to win, but only a few actually do. Does that mean everyone else is a loser?

Of course not! And Lombardi missed the point by just one word in another of his well-known quotes: *"I firmly believe that any man's finest hour, the greatest fulfillment of all that he holds dear, is that moment when he has worked his heart out in a good cause and lies exhausted on the field of battle – **victorious**."*

Lombardi came oh so close to "getting it."

Though his quote is profound and on the mark, he couldn't resist reverting back to his playbook of life. In essence, he qualified everything he said about what make a man's finest hour on whether or not he was ultimately victorious.

The reality of life is exactly the opposite of what Lombardi said. A man is victorious when he has fought the good fight.

A man is victorious when he has worked his heart out for a good cause and lies exhausted on the field of battle.

Those two traits, and those two alone, are what defines a man's greatest hour, the greatest fulfillment of all he holds dear.

Coach Lombardi had nothing over Danny Bukantz's son when it came to wanting to win.

Danny Bukantz's son won. He won because he tried his best out of unending love for his dad.

While I was immersed in the journey, it was nearly impossible to understand that. In reality, nearly everything I did was focused on winning. For three decades, it was win, win, win. It didn't matter that I was trying to follow in Dad's footsteps. It didn't matter what extra incentive and motivation I had.

What mattered is that, to me, winning wasn't the only thing, it was *everything*.

I felt that in order to follow in Dad's footsteps, I'd have to duplicate Dad's tangible accomplishments. Nothing else mattered. It didn't matter how I got there; it only mattered *that* I got there.

Wow, was that a myopic outlook. I had become the poster boy for the cliché "can't see the forest from the trees."

And then it hit me. It hit me square between the eyes. I had it all wrong. I always had.

In an ironic twist of poetic justice, I was struck by a lightning bolt that came from one of the darkest clouds in my life: Albie Axelrod.

My love for Dad was rivaled only by my disdain for Axelrod. I can't deny it. I can't pretend it didn't exist. There is no way to sugarcoat it.

When I looked at the disparity between these two American fencing icons, there wasn't much difference except for Axelrod's Olympic bronze medal.

Actually, that wasn't the difference at all.

Why exactly did I strive to be like my dad? Why exactly did I strive not to be like Axelrod?

As I've said earlier, Axelrod defined his status as a person based on that prestigious piece of bronze. Sadly, he never received the adulation and respect he coveted more than anything. He thought the medal made the man. The stark reality is that he proved he was better than most on the fencing strip. He thought his success as a competitor superseded whatever attributes he had as a regular person. Unfortunately, he never understood that he was really perceived by how he acted off of the fencing strip.

He never understood that a person can never be defined by the hardware.

Well, okay, that was pretty simple; why, then, did I want to be like Dad so much? The whole story about my journey revolved around tangible feats:

Could I win a National Championship – like Dad?

Could I make an Olympic Team – like Dad?

Could I win the Maccabiah gold medal – like Dad?

Could I referee in the Olympics – like Dad?

Would I ever be elected into a Hall of Fame – like Dad?

I spent thirty-plus years training, traveling, and sacrificing for those tangible things. After all, I wanted to be like my dad. I wanted to follow in his footsteps.

And you know what? I, like Axelrod, was focused on the wrong stuff.

I was so proud of my dad because of his great accomplishments in the sport. But I didn't love him for that. No, sir! I loved Dad, but not for his press clippings and medals; I loved him because of the wonderful man that he was.

There is a reason Dad has so many friends around the world. There is a reason that he earned the love and respect of everyone. It isn't because he won fencing bouts…

It's because he won hearts.

So for more than thirty years, I pursued the wrong dream. While it was a worthwhile journey, for what I thought was a noble cause, I finally figured out there was a far nobler cause.

And that was to strive to be like my dad – as a person.

Well, when I think about it, that would have been a lot harder than making four Olympic Teams!

After all, Danny Bukantz's son turned out to be "The John McEnroe of Fencing."

25

The Hardest Footstep to Follow

Every set of footsteps has ten toes. In the previous chapter I listed nine of my dad's accomplishments, which represent nine of those ten toes I had to fill. There was a tenth toe, of course, that I would also have to accomplish for myself. However, unlike the other feats that were black and white and tangible, the tenth was something that fell into the gray zone. It was this tenth toe that I recounted in his IJSHF induction speech for him, one that epitomizes his strong character.

Remember when I told you that an athlete's success isn't about the hardware, but the software?

There is a story about Danny Bukantz that trivializes his thirteen US National Championships and nine Olympic Games. It's a story that, on the surface, seems like a tall tale. But it actually happened, and it says much more about him and his software than all of his gold medals put together.

At the 1964 Tokyo Olympics, the men's saber semifinal was between Poland and the Soviet Union. In addition to being a match between the two best teams, with only one moving on to the gold medal bout, it was a match that was destined to be a bloodbath for reasons that obviously had nothing to do with sport.

The occupied Poles wanted to extract their revenge in the worst way; the Soviets would be sent to Siberia if they lost. In addition, the Soviets were afraid (or paranoid) that an unfriendly or sympathetic referee would favor the Poles, the underdog (in more ways than one).

The Soviets told the bout committee that they would only agree to one referee. Incredibly, that referee was from the country in the midst of a Cold War with the Soviet Union. They requested, and would only accept, Danny Bukantz.

Mark Rakita, an Olympic gold medalist on that Soviet saber team event in 1964, said to me decades later, "Your father was the only referee in the world who we could trust."

That's something you can't put in a medal case or scrapbook.

That intangible quality – *integrity* – is the tenth and final toe in my dad's enormous footsteps. How the hell would I ever live up to that? Would I ever be worthy of that kind of respect? Following in his footsteps sure was one giant pain in the ass! But, of course, I'd try.

In every walk of life, each person draws his or her own particular line in the sand. We do this in sports, business, relationships, etc. In life, it's inevitable that most people eventually cross the line they've drawn for themselves. We are, after all, human beings and we succumb to temptations; none of us is perfect.

I'll be the first to admit that I've crossed the line at times. But, for whatever reason, I decided early on in my fencing career that the one area of my life in which I could never cross the line would be when refereeing.

For the most part, referees are fair. That's the essence of being an "arbiter." However, some referees cross the line at times for various reasons. Remember what happened during the 1985 Maccabiah Games when I lost the important semifinal bout to Hatuel? I pray that I'm wrong on this one, but in my heart, I'm sure that the referee, Plasterie, gave the home team the benefit of the doubt – and the bout to the Israeli.

It may have been an honest mistake, or it may have been a subconscious decision. Hell! It may have been a conscious one, but who knows? I know Plasterie and like the guy, so I'm hoping it wasn't the latter.

At the 2004 Olympic Games in Athens, the Hungarian referee, Joszef Hidasi – his fifth Games as a referee! – was assigned to officiate the gold medal bout in men's foil between China and Italy. There's been a rumor circulating for years that Hidasi was in cahoots with the Italians. Why he was assigned to this particular bout is beyond me.

Though he was considered one of the best foil refs in the world, the perception others had of him was tainted; most people in the fencing community believed he had compromised his ethics along the way.

Sure enough, there were six consecutive close calls that went against the Chinese fencer. Everyone's fears about Hidasi were finally realized. He was removed from the bout and suspended by the FIE, an act that received worldwide press and negative attention in the International Olympic Committee's report on fencing from the Games.

Some referees just have a tendency to give the close calls to the bigger name, be it a team or individual. Some referees give more calls to the countries that are more likely to yell at them, such as France or Italy, thereby attempting to choose the path of least resistance. Whether conscious or subconscious, subtle or blatant, some referees just decide to cross the line. You probably understand now why the Soviets felt the way they did when they requested my dad. The fact that they asked for an American ref during the Cold War further illustrates how respected Danny Bukantz was for his integrity.

So here's my story:

At NACs, the top fencers from Canada also compete and

use the US points for their own standings. In other words, NACs are serious business for everyone, as teams are on the line for both countries.

While the United States and Canada are friendly neighbors, they're anything but when it comes to fencing. The relationship between the countries on the strip is more akin to that of the Soviets and the Poles in 1964. Quite frankly, the lion's share of the antipathy and chilliness originates from the north. When it comes to Canadian fencers, for reasons I'll never comprehend, they just don't like us. Maybe they're envious of our non-socialized, and far more efficient, health care system…whatever! I know we don't have a problem with them, at least not in the fencing community.

The Canadians always brought down one or two referees to the NACs. Naturally, all of the other refs were Americans. This boils down to the fact that the Canadians, in their bouts against one another or against an American, were usually refereed by an American. Sadly, but understandably (I guess), they developed a complete distrust for the American refs. They typically felt that in any bout against an American, the American referee would give all the close calls to his or her countryman. As a fencer who has competed in many foreign countries, I fully empathize with the Canadians' point of view. I've been robbed blind in these exact same situations by hometown refs.

It's an inherent conflict of interest, but there are no other available options at the NACs. The US supplies the majority of the referees, and that's just the way it goes. It comes with the turf, which unfortunately led to a tiff with our northern neighbors.

During my heyday as a referee, the three top Canadian foilists were Luc Rocheleau, Benoit Giasson, and Stephan Angers. At least one, if not all three, would generally make it into the top eight at every NAC, and they would inevitably draw an American fencer. They also more than likely had to deal with an American referee. The Canadians hated this ever-present dynamic; when put into this situation, they often felt like they had two opponents to overcome. They had every right to feel that way, no matter how honest and fair the referee was.

Perception is reality. And the reality is it's human nature to perceive that a referee will help the fencer from his or her own country.

At the time, I was a competitor first at the NACs and a referee second. If I didn't make the finals, I'd offer up my officiating services. Sometimes the head referee would accept my offer, and I'd head into the locker room to change into street clothes.

I wasn't always in such high demand. There were plenty of times when I was eliminated just before the finals, after which the head ref would reason that I might be too tired and would simply say, "Thanks, but no thanks." In those instances, I'd hang around in my sweats and watch the finals because there were always at least one or two Fencers Club teammates still competing. I'd root them on and offer tactical advice from the side of the strip.

At one NAC in Chicago back in 1986, I was knocked out in the last bout before the finals. Because I hadn't trained at all that season before the national events, I was really wiped out. I offered my services but was turned down by George Kolombatovich, the competition's head referee. "Jeff," he answered, "I appreciate it, but you're dead tired and it wouldn't be fair to the refs we hired who've been working all day."

One of the bouts in the finals that day was slated to be between Stephan Angers, a Canadian, and Jack Tichacek, one of my Fencers Club teammates. Before the bout, Angers made it known that he was unhappy with the American referees Kolombatovich had selected for the finals. Now, in my opinion, that falls into the category of "tough luck, pal!" Seriously, no fencer should be in the position of telling the head referee which refs are acceptable and which aren't.

The tail can't wag the dog. Do you think basketball coach Bobby Knight – no matter how much he yells, no matter how big of a bully he is, no matter how big a jerk he is – is able to dictate to the NCAA which refs will officiate Texas Tech's games?

Of course not! And that's the way it has to be.

However, the NACs have a very specific and special problem. At a World Cup, it's prohibited for a referee to officiate a bout involving his or her country. Now this rule makes perfect sense. As I explained, NACs have a majority of American and only a handful of Canadian referees. If a competition only had one or two Canadian referees, there's absolutely no way the head ref would assign them to a Canadian bout unless it was between two Canadian fencers.

Angers refused to back down and continued to badger Kolombatovich, who could have easily blown Angers off. But Kolombatovich understood Angers' stance and attempted to put out the fire.

So he asked Angers, "Okay, Stephan, instead of telling me who you won't accept for your bout, tell me who you would accept."

As the story was related to me, Angers immediately pointed in my direction and answered, "Jeff."

"But Jeff and Tichacek are from the same club," Kolombatovich warned.

"So what? He's the best and I trust him," Angers replied.

So there I was… in my sweats, unshaven, (that's right, Mom!) and, after not having officiated a single bout the entire day, I was plucked from the sidelines and thrown into the fray. I was an American handpicked by a Canadian to officiate a bout between him and an American fencer from my club.

With that gesture by Angers and with those words – "… and I trust him" – I had followed in my dad's footsteps.

And this meant more to me than all the medals, awards, and national and international teams combined.

26

How Sweet It Is

I never got to see my dad compete, as he retired when I was about four or five years old.

Fortunately, I was able to find a 16MM film of Dad fencing Buhan at the FC exhibition and, thanks to Skip Shurtz, also fencing Mangiarotti at the 1956 Olympics. I was lucky enough to watch him referee and pattern my officiating style and bedside manner after him. When I look back, however, two of the most memorable moments I've had were when Dad was inducted into the CCNY Sports Hall of Fame in 1967 and when I gave a speech in his absence at the induction into the International Jewish Sports Hall of Fame in 2001.

As I wrote earlier, after I won the gold medal in foil at the Maccabiah Games in 1989, my good buddy Eric Rosenberg wasted no time in joking, "West Essex Jewish Sports Hall of Fame, here we come!"

It was really funny at the time, because while there were quite a few Jewish Sports Halls of Fame, there were none in New Jersey. Well, wouldn't you know that sometime in 2003,

I received a call from a Maccabiah friend, world-class golfer Jay Blumenfeld, asking me to join him on a committee for the newly formed Metrowest JCC Sports Hall of Fame. When I said yes, I burst out laughing at the thought of Rosenberg's tongue-in-cheek crack coming to fruition.

When I joined the committee, which was chaired by Jay, I looked forward to helping find the most qualified Jewish athletes in New Jersey. At that time I hadn't even thought about getting in, at least not for many years. My philosophy has always been that the Hall should first honor the qualified old-timers so they could enjoy it while they're still with us.

The youngsters, myself included, could wait.

Sure enough, there was a plethora of older and deceased great Jewish athletes from New Jersey, particularly from the Newark area. There were pro baseball players, pro football players, pro basketball players, famous boxers who competed for world championships, legendary coaches from Weequahic High School, and a whole host of others. While I hadn't heard of most of these people, I was enthralled to see how others on the committee who had grown up in this area talked about the athletes with reverence.

Evidently, there were many legends – Jewish sports legends – from New Jersey.

While the committee was formed in 2003, the first class would be inducted in August of 2004, just before the start of the Athens Olympics. As the meetings progressed, the committee basically whittled down the list to a handful of those who would become first ballot automatics. I was once asked to leave the room while the committee discussed my name. My good buddy Bob Largman had sent in my nomination. I immediately told the committee that I would prefer they save me for a later year so a deserving old-timer could be honored. While I won't deny for a single second that I would have been thrilled beyond belief to be elected in the Hall's inaugural year, I honestly meant what I said.

And here's why.

To this day it burns me that Dad has yet to be elected into the New York Jewish Sports Hall of Fame at the Suffolk YMHA in Long Island. Can you imagine that he is in the International Jewish Sports Hall of Fame but not yet in the New York Hall? And, to add insult to insult, the New York Hall not only puts in those with substantially lesser credentials, but also many youngsters.

So while selection to these Halls will always be highly subjective based on either what you've done or who you know, in my opinion, an objective criterion should be set to honor the senior living legends first. Certainly, active athletes should not be eligible.

Anyway, I nominated Dad for both the IJSHOF and the NYJSHOF way back in 1993. As of 2006, he's still not in the small one. You do the math.

As opposed to bashing the credibility of the New York Hall (as they've done it themselves…), I decided to learn from its mistakes. I promised to stand by my principles while on the committee of the New Jersey Hall.

"Thanks for considering me," I said, "I'm flattered. But I'll wait my turn."

Jay thanked me, but replied, "Jeff, please leave the room so we can at least have an open discussion, okay?"

So I went out into the hallway at the JCC, paced for about twenty minutes, completely conflicted because I really wanted to get in. Would it really be that terrible if a relative youngster (at forty-six years old) was elected?

It just seemed that there was a hurdle at every turn throughout my entire fencing career. First as a slow-developing fencer, then with the roadblock I ran into in my international refereeing, and now, would it be because I was too young?

As I kept pacing in the hallway of the Metrowest JCC, I had resigned myself to waiting for this honor a few more years.

And then, Jay came out to get me. "You're in," he said with a huge smile.

"You're kidding, right?" I asked, hoping he wasn't.

"No, seriously," he continued. "It was unanimous."

When I rejoined the committee, they told me that in order to get into the Hall, I'd have to officially resign from the committee for that year, so it wouldn't appear as if there was a conflict of interest.

"No, I'd prefer to stay on the committee," I joked.

Just kidding! I was numb and, as usual, choked up. My first thought was not the reality of getting in, but rather that both Mom and Dad would be there to share the evening with me. That meant more than anything.

The induction dinner was scheduled to take place on Monday, August 2nd at the Crestmont Country Club, about two miles from my house. That would be a true hall of fame week for me, as I was to depart for the Olympics in Athens three days later. There was no denying it or pooh-poohing it, this evening was to be a big night in my life.

Actually, the entire week was pretty much the culmination of a lifelong dream. The journey began for real in 1972 – the journey to follow in my dad's footsteps. It was a long and frustrating journey. I've learned in life that one must appreciate the journey, as there is never a guarantee of the hoped-for destination. However, if that destination is ever reached, you have to take a step back, appreciate the moment, and reflect.

After thirty-two years of riding a physical and emotional rollercoaster, the thrill-ride of a lifetime had brought me to that seemingly unreachable destination in August of 2004.

For me, making the US Olympic Team was always the ultimate dream. While it didn't turn into an absolute nightmare, as I was this close to making the team in 1984 and 1988, I fell just short. When I was selected by the USFA's High Performance Committee to be the 2004 Olympic Team captain, that was good enough for me. Maybe I wasn't a competitor, but I still was an integral part of the team. Best of all, it counted as a footstep fulfilled.

As for ever making it into any Hall of Fame – that was something I never expected. So when it came to be, I was quite surprised. That evening at the Crestmont Country Club would prove to be a great one for me, as many family and friends came to share it with me.

Appropriately, the first two fencers my dad ever watched me fence (and get beaten by), Mitch Dorfman and Eric Rosenberg, were there. My beloved coach Simon Pinkhasov was there. "Uncle" Chaba Pallaghy, long past the insult of 1988, was there. Jack Tichacek, who had become a really good friend of mine since we'd retired from competitive careers, was there. Old Fencers Club friends Bill Mindel and Wilma Friedman were there.

Even my old Camp Scatico buddies, Ben Krull and Elisa and Mike Madorsky, were there. My golfing partners, Mark Kempner, Steve Waxgiser, and Les "Moondog" Melnick were there. Old work friends Larry Tepper and Norm Lehrer were there. Toni Wortman, the President of Maccabi USA/Sports for Israel, was there. Of course, my family came out to be with me. Carol, Stephanie, Uncle Bob, and cousins Mike, Keith, and Lori were there.

The only person missing was my son Michael, as he was up at Camp Scatico. (Don't worry, Michael, I'd have stayed at camp, too!)

To make the evening absolutely perfect, Mom and Dad were there – and looked fantastic. "Jeffrey, darling, how do I look tonight?" Mom asked.

"Mom," I said, "you've never looked better!"

But there was an aspect of that evening that proved to be the icing on the cake. Prior to being called up to give the induction speech, each inductee would be introduced by someone. For me, that "someone" was to be the man whose legacy I'd been chasing and whom I revered.

Dad was called up, spoke emotionally for a couple minutes, and then introduced me. At that moment, what can I say, time stood still.

I don't remember much of what he said, and I wasn't thinking about what I was about to say in my speech. As I walked up to the podium, all I could think of was that it was so cool and moving to have Dad up there with me. We hugged, I probably got choked up again, and Dad presented me with the award plaque. We posed for a few photos. Those fleeting moments will forever be imbedded in my mind.

If it were up to me, I would have just asked Dad to stay up there with me instead of giving my speech. Nobody in the audience would have remembered one word I said anyway. Maybe, just maybe, they would have understood the love I had for my dad.

My big night was eerily similar to Dad's big night in January 1967 at the inaugural CCNY Hall of Fame induction. Had it really been thirty-seven years since that night?

There was one major difference, though.

At his dinner, he was proud to have represented his school and proud of his accomplishments. On this night, it was far more emotional for me. Of course, I was incredibly proud to have been elected, let alone in the inaugural induction to this Hall. Of course, I was so honored to have my family and friends share it with me.

Best of all, I had this indescribable feeling of having followed in Dad's footsteps and of having him there to present me with the award he inadvertently caused me to pursue for most of my life.

In the world of fencing, I was no longer just Danny Bukantz's son.

I had come full circle. I entered this world on September 17, 1957 as a premature and jaundiced five-pound little chicken, so tiny that Mom used to bathe me in a stewing pot.

But this little five-pound kid was born with a two hundred-pound chip on his shoulder, as I would forever be known in the fencing world as *Danny Bukantz's son*.

I spent most of my life trying to fill Dad's footsteps and become known within the fencing world as *Jeff Bukantz*.

It was the journey of a lifetime, replete with the lowest of lows and the highest of highs.

There were self-doubts throughout the whole ride, as I always feared I'd fail to fill Dad's footsteps.

For over three decades, I kept trying to close the distance to Dad's legacy, and transform myself in the sport from Danny Bukantz's son to just Jeff Bukantz.

Then, through the perseverance instilled in me by Mom, I somehow reached my destination.

I had filled Dad's footsteps. I had earned my own name in the sport.

And then… it hit me.

If I had failed to fill Dad's footsteps, it wouldn't have mattered. That I tried my best is all that mattered. Win or lose, I was still going to be known in the sport as Jeff Bukantz.

When I realized that I embarked on a three-decade journey primarily out of love for my dad, I decided that I'd forever want to be known in fencing as Danny Bukantz's son.

All those years of closing the distance brought me right back to where I was to begin with… and where I always wanted to be… just *Danny Bukantz's son*.

And you know what? I always thought that was pretty cool.

Acknowledgements

Many friends and family have played a major role in the success I've enjoyed. Without their support, I may have ended the journey and never reached the destination.

If not for **Lenny Messitte** calling my "fat ass" out of gym class, I may have never even started my career on the Forest Hills High School team. Lenny knew little about fencing, but he knew plenty about leading and inspiring know-it-all teenagers. Coach "Mo" – short for "momentum" – led us to the city championship match against powerhouse Stuyvescent in the fall of 1972.

Along the way I trained with many coaches. Each one, in his own way, contributed to my fencing style.

I was extremely fortunate to have started with the late **Michel Alaux**, who trained one of the greatest foilists in history, Frenchman Christian D'Oriola. Our relationship was cut short in 1974 when Michel passed away from lung cancer.

After Michel's passing, I trained for a while with **Herb Cohen**. Herb was the only lefty coach I ever had (other than my dad), and that turned out to be a blessing. Early in my career, I was psyched out against fellow left-handers. Herb worked with me on lefty-to-lefty actions, and I developed not only the moves, but the confidence to overcome the fear of lefties forever.

At Penn State, **Coach Maxwell (Mac) Garret** taught me a lesson more important than any fencing action. As an immature seventeen-year-old, I complained about every little injury. Mac pointed out to me that teammate Mitch Dorfman, who was in and out of the hospital for an entire year after a near-fatal bicycle accident, never said a word. After that reality check, I learned to put things in perspective.

The late **Csaba Elthes** was the fencing master who helped me turn the corner. Csaba, a Hungarian legend known for whipping his students across their legs when they made mistakes during their lessons – often drawing blood – instilled a discipline that I had previously lacked as a fencer.

But Csaba never hit me. It wasn't as if I didn't make plenty of mistakes in the thrice-weekly lessons, so why was I spared? I finally figured it out: Dad worked on Csaba's teeth, which evidently worked to my advantage. Csaba was responsible for my emergence on the national scene.

After Csaba suffered a stroke, I began a relationship with **Semyon (Simon) Pinkhasov** that lasts until this day. At the time, Dad considered Simon to be the best foil coach in the country. Simon came to the United States in 1977 from Moscow, learned the language, got his physical therapy degree, and coached more top foilists than any other coach in the US. In 1983, Simon was offered the job of Head Coach at Princeton University, a plum job for any coach. Incredibly, he turned down the position, as he didn't want to let down his students who were in the running for the 1984 Olympic Games. Simon coached me through my best years, and one of my career highlights was being together with him on the 1987 Pan American Games Team.

Eric Rosenberg and I had quite an auspicious initial meeting in 1972, to say the least. Eric led the Cardozo High School fencing team's mantra to "kick the fat ass of Danny Bukantz's son," and he did, indeed, do just that. Worst of all, it was the first time Dad ever saw me fence competitively. We became friends a few years later and shared many wonderful moments together around the country and the world. My career was graced by the fact that Dogbreath and I were able to compete together on the US National Championship Teams and World Maccabiah Teams.

Eric taught me that it was impossible to be loved by everybody, and was always there for me when the chips were down.

Carl Borack and I also met in 1972, albeit at the Olympics Games in Munich, where he was competing. Our next meeting was in 1987, when Carl was my Team Captain of the US Pan American Games Team. We probably didn't become friends until almost twenty years later when we both served on the USFA's International Selection Committee. While Carl became my trusted confidant in fencing, he was thrust into the unenviable position of having me replace him as Team Captain, a position he held for over four quadrennials. It must have been very difficult for Carl to pass the torch after devoting the majority of the last eighteen years on the job, but he went out of his way to mentor and support me.

Stacey Johnson changed my life. When Stacey became USFA President in 2000, I was at risk of becoming a political outcast in the sport. (I had acquired a few enemies... I also had a propensity for taking no prisoners when I spoke my mind.) Stacey believed in me, nominated me for the FIE (International Fencing Federation) Rules Commission, put me back on the USFA's Fencing Officials Commission, and also kept me on the USFA's International Selection Committee. She had the courage to tell me that I had to soften my act and clear the air with my enemies. After initially resisting (I was, after all the John McEnroe of Fencing), I took Stacey's heartfelt advice. The end result was that by the end of her term, I went from being an unpopular hot potato to having to decide between remaining Team Captain or taking over for Stacey as USFA President.

Thanks to Stacey, even my once-mortal enemies supported me for the Presidency, which was nothing short of mind-boggling. I owe my emergence as a leader to the trust Stacey had in me and to the wisdom she imparted on me.

Chaba Pallaghy and Dad were good friends and often roomed together when they traveled around the world as referees. Uncle Chaba would eventually become one of my mentors and, despite the generational difference, great friends.

Although we did butt heads – especially when I deeply insulted him by quitting as an international referee in 1988 – Uncle Chaba was there for me when I decided to go for the 1996 Olympics as a ref.

Uncle Chaba taught me about refereeing, politics, people, respect, and sticking to one's principles regardless of the potential political fallout. I'm honored that Uncle Chaba anointed me as one of his 'sons.'

From 1981 until 1994, I was the only member of the New York Fencers Club to represent the foil team at every National Championship. Without a doubt, being part of that team was one of the most meaningful and memorable experiences of my career. While I am proud to have been a member of eight National Championship Teams, and to follow in Dad's footsteps, I'll always be most grateful for the friendships that will last a lifetime.

Thanks to my great FC teammates **Eric Rosenberg, Jack Tichacek, Michael McCahey, John Nonna, Lew Siegel, Jerome DeMarque, Dr. Nathaniel Cohen, Phil Mathis, John Troiano, Peter Lewison, Al Carlay, Rob Conway, Philippe Bennett,** and **Dan Kellner.** Special thanks to **Semyon Pinkhasov,** who coached thirteen of the fifteen fencers who represented the FC during the eight-championship run. **Go FC!**

Sam Cheris and I had a rocky start back in the early 1980s. It was inevitable, as I often refereed for Sam's wife Elaine. However, we eventually served together for many years on the USFA's International Selection Committee and the Fencing Official's Commission. In fact, it was Sam who proposed me for Chair of the FOC, a position that I held for three years, where I first gained the confidence to lead a group within the organization.

Once, in a hotly contested ISC meeting, I fought tooth and nail on possibly the least significant agenda item. I won, but as Sam said to me afterward, "At what cost?" Thanks to

Sam, I learned to pick my spots or risk falling on deaf ears on the most important issues.

The late **Bill Goering** was my biggest supporter during my three-year Chairmanship of the Fencing Officials Commission. When others were sniping or criticizing, Bill always made sure to send me a private email telling me to stick to my guns. I'll always remember Bill's unyielding integrity.

I met **Tommy Rosenberg** in 1974, but it wasn't in the fencing world. Instead, we were counselors at Camp Scatico in Elizaville, New York. Over the last thirty plus years, Tommy has become one of my dearest friends. He has always been a giving person. At Scatico, he 'gave' me a Color War victory when we were opposing Generals of the Grey and Green teams. Also at Scatico, he gave me the opportunity to name him a 'Pencil Neck Geek.'

Seriously, Tommy has always been there for me, whether it was with legal support, moral support, or athletic support. I'll never forget when he and his wife Karen drove to Indianapolis from Columbus, Ohio in 1987 to attend the Opening Ceremonies of the Pan American Games.

Although I'm an only child, Tommy will always be like a brother to me.

Mark (Big Poppa) Kempner has been there for me through thick and thin. Whenever the going got tough, Kemp was there to prop me up. When I lapsed into feeling sorry for myself, he always gave me the necessary reality check to help me right the ship. That's what friends are for, and I'm very lucky to call Kemp my true-blue friend.

Terrence Gargiulo has been a good friend and mentor. Terrence propped me up when I was down, encouraged me to utilize my 'chutzpah,' and always kept me focused.

Cousin Mike Omansky was like a brother to me. Always upbeat, always supportive, and even acted as ring announcer at my Maccabiah Games pro wrestling fundraiser.

Norman Lehrer, another non-fencer (or civilian, as I like to call them), and I worked together for many years. Norm and I played indoor tennis for many years until he asked me to play with his son Ben, a member of the Columbia High School (in New Jersey) team.

When I returned home from the 2005 World University Games in late August, I found out that my buddy Norm was diagnosed with stage-four lung cancer and given six months to two years to live. If there really was a God, this wouldn't have happened to such a decent man. But Norm has played the tough hand by battling and showing tremendous courage. Norm's sheer determination and positive attitude has been an inspiration to all of his friends, and we pray for his full recovery.

My mom's younger brother, **Robert Ellyn (Uncle Bob)**, is an amazing man. Uncle Bob, also a Holocaust survivor, has encountered family tragedy that tested his will. Uncle Bob's love of life and the attitude that he will persevere through the darkest times has been simply remarkable. While he has joked that he must be a cat, as he's used up about nine lives, Uncle Bob has had the spirit and courage of nine people.

Uncle Bob didn't partake in Steven Spielberg's Shoah project documenting the taped stories of survivors because he didn't want to relive that unspeakable experience. Instead of humanizing and glorifying Black September terrorists, as he did in *Munich*, Spielberg really should tell the true story about this incredible man's will to live, no matter the obstacles.

Uncle Bob, you are a pillar of strength and virtue, and deserving of more love than you can imagine.

Without the guidance and input of my editors, **Allison Rowland** and **Elizabeth Nollner**, this memoir couldn't have happened. Allison is now a civilian, but was once a fencer. She helped me narrow my focus of the last thirty plus years, allowed me to write in my own style, and gave her objective opinions throughout the entire process. Thanks to Allison and Elizabeth's TLC, I hope this book painted a picture that depicted a son's lifelong journey to follow in his father's footsteps.

Paige Stover Hague has been my beacon of hope as I entered the world of professional speaking. The writing of this book was her impetus, and without Paige's ever-present positive attitude and cheerful outlook, I definitely wouldn't have gotten this far.

Juanell Teague and **James Huggins** believed in me, supported me, and encouraged me to tell my stories.

Last, but not least, I come to my immediate family. My wonderful children, **Stephanie** and **Michael**, accepted the fact that their father would be away for many weekends and even for quite a few two-week trips. I am so proud of both of you for your maturity, discipline, and success in every aspect of your lives. Sometimes I want to check your DNA just to make sure you both really came from me.

If you are half as proud of me as I am of you, I am a very lucky Dad.

My wife **Carol** probably didn't know what she was getting herself into when we married in 1982. But she found out right away, as we had to postpone our honeymoon when the dates of the 1982 US Nationals were changed from late June to late May… after we had planned our wedding. When I broke the news to Carol in our West Orange apartment, she was incredulous and asked, "Do you mean to say you love fencing more than you love me?"

Fortunately, I ducked and the frying pan missed my head as it whizzed past it.

Fencing was destined to dominate much of my life, and I know it was unfair to the entire family, but especially to Carol. Whether it was for refereeing, competing, attending USFA meetings, or acting as Team Captain, I was away a lot. Without Carol's support, no matter how resentful she must have been, I wouldn't have been able to enjoy such a lengthy and varied career in the sport.

Carol, you have been the best friend, the best mother, and the glue of our family.

About the Author

Jeff Bukantz was born in Forest Hills, New York, and grew up in a legendary fencing family. His father, Danny Bukantz, competed in four Olympic Games (1948, '52, '56, and '60), and won four US National Individual Foil Championships during his storied fencing career.

Through practice and persistence Jeff eventually became a legitimate contender like his father, generally ranking 5th or 6th in the country. He qualified for the 1981 World University Games Team and the 1983 and 1987 World Championship Teams. In 1987 he competed at the Pan American Games, where he won a bronze medal for the US team. Jeff completed a long personal journey by winning a gold medal two years later at the 1989 World Maccabiah Games. He also won many titles back home, including eight US National Foil Team Championships for the New York Fencers Club.

Jeff's journey to become an Olympian like his father was long and difficult, as he was the third alternate for both the 1984 and 1988 Olympic Games. In 1984 he refereed at the Olympic Games in Los Angeles, and in 1996 at the Men's Individual Foil Finals in Atlanta. On December 26, 2003 Jeff received word that the US Fencing Association had selected him to captain the 2004 US Olympic Fencing Team – an honor he had wanted to share with his father for over thirty years.

To learn more about Jeff, or to book him for a speaking program at your organization, please visit www.JeffBukantz.com.